빠르고 정확한 독해를 위한

Just
READING

3

혁신 개정판
Just Reading 3

지은이 신석영
발행인 조상현
발행처 (주)위아북스

주소 서울시 마포구 마포대로 127. 304호
문의 02-725-9988 **팩스** 02-725-9863
등록번호 제300-2007-164호
홈페이지 www.wearebooks.co.kr
ISBN 978-89-6614-043-5 53740

혁신 개정판

빠르고 정확한 독해를 위한

Just
READING

신석영 지음

3

We're
위아북스

PROLOGUE

　"꿈에 젖은 수년보다 강렬한 한 시간이 더 많은 것을 이룬다."라는 말이 생각납니다. 지금 누구보다도 강렬한 인생을 살고 있는 사람은 학생들이 아닌가 싶습니다. 대학을 목표로 열심히 공부하는 학습자들에게는 공부를 잘하는 방법과 어떻게 준비하고 대처를 해야 좋은 점수를 받을 수 있을까? 하는 의문과 절실함은 항상 변함이 없습니다. 똑같은 노력과 주어진 시간이 같다면 좀 더 효과적으로 공부할 수 있도록 도움을 줄 수 있는 안내자와 같은 좋은 책과 선생님들이 절실히 필요할 때입니다. "한 권의 책이 사람의 인생을 바꿀 수도 있다"는 말이 있습니다.

　이 책은 저자가 직접 현장에서 오랜 세월동안 직접 가르치며 만들었습니다. 아이들과 함께 울고, 웃고, 기뻐하며 힘들고 행복했던 시간들을 함께 하면서 조금씩 다듬어 나갔습니다.

　힘든 곳과 아픈 곳을 직접 어루만지며 또한 학생들에게서 더 많은 가르침을 받은 저자가 학생들의 어려움을 해소할 수 있도록 심혈을 기울였습니다.

　영어를 잘 듣고, 말하고, 쓰기 위해서는 많이 읽어야 합니다. 영어는 읽어 이해할 수 있는 속도와 정확도의 범위만큼만 들리며, 읽은 내용이 숙지되면 회화가 이루어지고, 글로 표현하면 영작문이 따라오게 됩니다. 독해영역이 상당히 별개의 분야처럼 이해되어 회화와 영작이 별도의 훈련이 필요한 것처럼 여겨져 왔는데, 이와 같은 고정관념을 깨는 대 수술이 필요합니다. 크라센(Crashen)이라는 언어학자는 '많이 읽을 것'을 강조합니다. 그는 배경지식을 알고, 읽어서 이해할 수 있는 영문을 많이 읽는 것이 영어 정복의 지름길임을 지적합니다. 오늘날 싱가포르의 영어 실력이 이를 증명하는데, 싱가포르의 리콴유 전 총리는 학교 교실 뒤에 영문서적을 수십, 수백 권을 비치해두고 읽기 교육을 시켰습니다. 우리나라는 우선 말해야 한다는 강박관념에 사로잡혀 읽기 교육이 제대로 안 되고 있는 현실입니다.

　대학 수학능력 시험과 TOEFL, TOEIC과 같은 시험에서의 관건은 다양한 지문을 얼마나 많이 접하고 또 얼마나 빨리 이해하느냐에 달려있습니다. 가장 좋은 방법은 쉬운 지문부터 단계별로 공부하면서 영어 독해와 영작 그리고 듣기에 대한 자신감을 가지도록 하는 것입니다. 그런데 현재 영어 교육은 학습자 중심이 아닌 현실과 동떨어져 있고 학습자에 대한 세심한 배려나 사랑이 없어 보입니다. 학습자들은 처음부터 어려운 지문을 접하게 되거나,

흥미 없는 소재를 바탕으로 단계학습을 하게 되는데, 이는 영어를 몇 년을 배워도 투자한 시간과 노력에 비하여 드러나는 학습효과가 실로 미미합니다. 이에 따라, 학생들은 영어가 주는 재미를 느낄 수 없을 뿐 아니라, 오히려 스트레스만 늘어갈 뿐입니다. 당연히 학교시험과 '영어 자체'에는 늘 자신 없어 합니다.

Just Reading 시리즈는 이런 학생들을 위해 정밀하게 제작된 Reading 교재입니다. 수능과 TOEFL, TOEIC에 맞춘 지문과 문제는 학생들에게 실제적인 도움을 줄 것입니다.

사실, 이 책을 쓴 저자의 목표와 이상은 더 높은 곳에 있습니다. 우리가 안고 있는 근본적인 문제는 학습 분위기 저변에 깔린 비판적 성향과 고정된 사고방식, 그리고 검증되지 않은 낡은 선입견들입니다. 한 언어가 자리 잡기 위해서는 다양한 작업이 요구되는데 그 중 가장 중요한 부분은 실제 많은 훈련을 할 수 있는 빈도와 학습자의 자신감입니다.

언어는 말이요, 말은 정신이요, 정신은 사상입니다. 사상은 인격을 만듭니다. 생소한 언어체계가 우리의 뇌에 자리 잡기까지 글로 된 많은 양의 독서를 필요로 합니다. 이 책에서 학습자들이 다양한 범 교과서적인 소재를 읽고 즐기는 동시에 많은 도움 장치들로 구성되어 있음을 밝혀 둡니다. 단순한 대학입시가 목적이 아닌 하나의 과정으로 더 큰 꿈과 미래를 향해 나아갈 대한민국 모든 학생들에게 응원을 보냅니다.

"Just Reading 혁신 개정판"이 출간되기까지 더 좋은 책을 위해 헌신의 노력을 다해주신 위아북스 관계자 여러분들에게 고개 숙여 깊은 감사를 드립니다. 마지막으로 항상 옆에서 힘이 되어주는 내 가족, 힘이 들 때마다 묵묵히 응원해준 내 아내 미선이, 그리고 아빠에게 언제나 용기와 희망을 주는 서윤이와 강민이에게 끝없는 사랑과 감사를 전합니다.

신석영

ABOUT Reading 1

독해를 위한 공부 방법

"독해력이란?"

독해력은 'Reading Power' 즉, '읽어 이해할 수 있는 능력'을 말한다. 많은 학생들이 '독해'가 무엇인지를 물어보면 십중팔구 읽고 해석하는 것, 읽고 번역하는 것이라 한다. 지금까지 수능, 토익, 토플 같은 시험에서는 한번도 '읽고 해석'하는 시험을 낸 적이 없다. 'Reading Comprehension' 즉, 읽고 이해하는 것이 독해이다. 단지 단어를 외워 단어만 읽어나가려고 한다. 그러나 reading의 첫 출발은 '글을 쓴 작가의 의도'를 파악하는 것, 즉, 글을 통하여 작가의 중요한 생각(Main idea)을 알아 내가는 힘이 '독해력'이며 고난도 독해력 측정이라는 것은 이러한 글의 중요성을 파악하고 추론해 내는 능력이 있는지를 측정하는 것을 가리킨다. 왜? Main idea를 통해 독해력을 측정하는 것일까? 이는 이러한 정도의 수준 높은 문제를 풀 줄 아는 학생이 대학의 학문을 이해할 수 있을 것으로 판단되기 때문이다.

1 이 글은 무엇에 관한 것인가?

주제문장(Topic Sentence/Main idea)이란, 주제(Topic)가 포함된 문장으로, 그 글이나 단락의 내용이 무엇에 관한 것인가를 함축적으로 대변하는 문장이다. 따라서, 이 주제 문장을 통해 글을 읽는 독자는 그 글이 어떤 내용인가를 예상할 수 있고, 글을 쓰는 작가는 하나의 생각(Idea)에 충실한 글을 쓸 수 있게 된다.

또한, 주제 문장은 사실(Fact)보다는 대개 글쓴이의 견해(Opinion)가 들어있는 문장으로, 주제(Topic)와 이를 제한 진술(Controlling statement)로 구성된다.

주제를 더욱 짧게 요약을 하게 되면 그것이 제목(Title)이 된다. 그 외에 Topic/Key Point 등으로 표현될 수 있다. 제목은 어떠한 글에서든지 지문을 중요한 하나의 요소로 통합시키는 것이 된다. 따라서 제목은 간단한 몇 단어로 나타내야 한다.

2 작가는 제목에 대해서 어떤 생각을 말하려고 하는가?

제목, 즉 글쓴이가 어떠한 것에 대해 말하려고 할 때, 그 말하려는 자신의 생각이 곧 주제(Main idea)가 된다. 이것은 주제문으로 표현이 되는데, 제목을 문장으로 나타내는 것이 주제문이다. '무엇이 어떠하다'라고 표현한다. 제목을 묻는 문제가 중요한 이유는 제목을 옳게 파악할 수 있다면 글의 중요한 요소를 파악하고 있는 것으로 볼 수 있기 때문이다.

3 자신의 생각을 어떻게 표현하는가?

　글쓴이는 반드시 글의 첫머리 부분에 '화젯거리'를 반드시 제시한다. '화젯거리(Controlling Statement)'는 마찬가지로 주제에 해당되는데 자신의 주장을 화젯거리로 제시하고, 이를 논리적으로 납득할 수 있는 다양한 설명으로 주제를 뒷받침해주는 문장들로 구성이 된다. 이러한 문장 구성 요소들을 'Supporting Sentences'라고 한다. 주제를 뒷받침해주는 보충, 부연 설명이 연이어 나오는데, 흔히 독해 문제에서 본문의 내용과 일치/불일치를 물어보는 문제는 이러한 세부적인 보충설명을 올바로 이해하는지를 측정하는 문제이다.

　전체 Supporting details(보충, 부연설명 문장)가 글의 주제와 논리적으로 잘 구성되어 하나의 흐름으로 연결이 잘 되었다면 이것을 우리는 '통일성'을 잘 갖춘 글이라고 한다. 문단은 하나의 주제문(Topic sentence)을 중심으로 하여 각 문장들이 주제문을 뒷받침하도록 관련성 있게 구성되어 있어야 한다. 비약을 하거나 논지에 어긋나는 문장이 나오는 경우가 있다. 이러한 문장은 제거하거나 수정해야 한다. 글쓰기와 교정 능력을 간접 평가하기 위해 자주 출제되고 있다.

4 내가 읽은 내용을 통해 어떤 결론을 추론해 낼 수 있는가?

　글의 도입부분에서 화젯거리, 즉 작가의 main idea를 파악하고 이것을 뒷받침해주는 보충, 부연 설명글을 모두 이해하고 나면 그 글에 대한 결론(Concluding Sentence)을 내릴 수 있어야 한다. 이때 결론은 글속에 제시되어 있을 수도 있고, 결론을 추론해 내야 하는 경우도 있다. 결론을 묻는 문제는 내가 파악이 가능했던 주제와 내용과 의미가 같아야 한다. 내가 읽은 내용과 거리가 멀다면 주제에서도, 결론에서도 벗어나 있다고 판단해야 한다. 함정 문제에서는 일반적인 타당성 있는 결론을 제시하기도 하는데, 반드시 글의 주제와 관련된 결론을 유추해 내야 하는 것이 중요하다.

A B O U T *Reading 2*

독해원리 정리

Paragraph 구성 원리

Main idea / Controlling statement 주제문
Support sentence
Support sentence
Support sentence
Support sentence
Support sentence
Concluding Sentence 결론 문장

① 하나의 단락(문단)은 몇 개의 문장이 모여 하나의 주제(핵심사상)를 다룬다.

② 단락은 일관된 하나의 주제와 그것을 보충 설명하는 문장들로 구성된다.

③ 보충 설명하는 문장을 다시 세부적으로 보충하거나, 예를 드는 문장이 있다.

※ 어떤 글에서, 글쓴이가 말하거나 설명하려는 것이 그 글의 주제(Main idea)가 된다. 이것은 글을 쓰는 사람의 입장에서 보면 글
쓴이가 말하고자 하는 것이 무엇인지를 전달하고 독자의 입장에서 보면 그 글이 무엇에 관한 것인지를 알게 한다.

Just Reading 시리즈의 특징

1 **각 Level별 25개의 실생활과 관련된 재미있는 독해 지문**

각 Level별 25개의 지문으로 구성되어 있으며, 5개의 지문이 하나의 Chapter로 이루어져 있다. 재미있는 주제와 다소 딱딱한 역사, 인물에 대한 지문까지 세밀화된 단계에 맞는 수준의 지문을 실었다. 유익한 지문을 통해 학생들은 다양한 시사, 문화, 역사, 인물, 사회, 과학 분야를 모두 배울 수 있도록 균형 있게 배치하였으며, 어떠한 유형의 독해 문제라도 당황하지 않고 대처할 수 있는 자기훈련의 기회를 제공하여 재미있게 공부할 수 있다.

2 **수능 기출 문제 수록**

각 Chapter별로 수능 기출 문제와 응용문제가 수록되어 있다. 특히 독해력을 측정하는 문제가 큰 비중을 차지하면서, 문제 출제도 사고력을 배양할 수 있도록 응용문제를 실어 원하는 대학 진학을 희망하는 학생들에게 도전정신과 자신감을 심어 줄 수 있도록 구성되었다.

3 **종합적 사고력, 분석력, 이해력을 획기적으로 길러 줄 참신한 문제**

화제와 주제 파악에 중점을 두되, 본문 내의 빈칸 추론하기, 요약하기, 어법(어휘) 문제, 논술형 문제, 결론 문제의 출제의도를 밝혀 놓아 독해력 측정의 여러 문제 유형에 자신 있게 대처할 수 있도록 하였다. 수능에 출제되는 모든 영역과 영어 제시문을 통해 각종 영어 시험에 대비할 수 있도록 구성되었다.

4 **지문을 난이도에 따라 적절히 배열**

각 Level을 세밀하게 나누어 영어에 대한 두려움을 쉽게 극복하도록 하였다. 각 Chapter별 마지막 지문은 200자 이상의 장문으로 구성하여 지문에 대한 종합적인 분석이 가능하게 하였고, Just Reading Series 3권에서는 장문이 2개씩 구성되어 풍부한 읽을거리를 통해 단계적인 실력 향상에 도움이 될 것이다.

5 **선생님·학생·학부모 모두가 참여할 수 있는 교재**

기존의 교재들은 항상 집필자가 이끌어가는 단방향적인 교재였으나 본 교재는 위 3자가 교재 중심으로 들어와서 서로 대화할 수 있도록 Daily Assignment Book을 Chapter별로 두어 학습의 효과를 높이도록 하였다.

6 **문장의 정확한 이해력을 바탕으로 Writing과 Speaking까지 완성**

기존의 책들은 독해 지문을 읽고 단순히 문제만 풀고 끝나는 구성인 반면 Just Reading은 공부한 독해 지문의 핵심 구문을 우리말과 영어를 비교분석하여 정확한 문장 이해력을 기른 후 영작으로 완성할 수 있도록 하였다. 또한 우리말로 완전히 이해한 영문구조를 이용하여 일상회화에서 자주 쓰이는 Speaking 스킬을 익힐 수 있도록 충분한 말하기 연습 활동을 구성하였다.

ABOUT *Just Reading Series* 2

Just Reading 구성의 특징

1 단원어휘 | Mini Quiz

각 Chapter에 필요한 단어를 미리 공부하고 스스로 테스트할 수 있도록 구성하였다. 단순한 암기보다는 collocation으로 의미 단위 어휘 확인이 가능하도록 하였다. 학생들은 단어를 지루하고 어려운 것이 아닌 '살아 있는 말'로 인식하게 될 것이며, 이러한 과정은 사고력 증진에 상당한 도움이 될 것이다.

2 독해에 진짜 필요한 Reading Skill

각 Chapter 마다 수능과 모든 독해에 필요한 독해 이론 수업이 마련되어 있다. 수능에 가장 많이 출제되는 단락의 구성 이론과 주제, 제목, 요지와 같은 유형을 모두 학습할 수 있다. 정보를 빨리 읽고 해석을 일일이 해내는 것도 중요하지만 이와 더불어 문장과 글의 논리를 정확하게 이해하는 '단락의 구성 이론'을 이해하는 능력도 반드시 필요하다.

3 Check Your Vocabulary!

보통의 책은 지문 밑에 단어 해설을 정리해 놓은 것이 보통이나, Just Reading 시리즈는 핵심 단어를 학생들이 스스로 조사해올 수 있도록 하였으며 이는 실제 수업에서 선생님이 숙제를 내주실 부분이다. 이렇게 하는 목적은 어휘는 한두 가지의 의미만을 내포하고 있는 것이 아닌 다양한 지문과 상황에 따라 그 의미가 결정되므로 독해 속 지문을 통해 학습자가 어휘의 뜻을 추론해보는 것 또한 사고력 향상을 위해 반드시 필요한 부분이기 때문이다.

4 구문으로 익히는 Writing & Speaking

'구문 독해 + 어휘 + 영작 + 해석연습'이 통합적으로 이루어지도록 구성하였다. 독해 해석 후 문제 풀이만 하면 끝나는 것이 아니라, 각 Unit마다 자가 학습 및 숙제를 내주어 학부형에게 확인을 받아 오는 시스템이다. 전통적인 문법이 아닌 현대식 영어로 영어와 한국어의 유사점을 비교·설명하여 우리나라 학습자들이 가장 난감해하는 영문 구조들을 확실하게 연습할 수 있다. 또한 우리말로 이해한 영어문장을 통해 실제 원어민이 자주 쓰는 스피킹 스킬을 읽힐 수 있다. 친구와 짝을 이루거나 그룹으로 말하기 연습을 할 수 있게 구성하여 학생들에게 흥미를 유발할 수 있는 수업을 할 수 있게 도움을 준다. 전국 어디에서도 찾아볼 수 없는 스피킹이 융합된 교재로 스피킹 시험 대비는 물론 말하기 능력 또한 향상시킬 수 있다.

5 WORD REVIEW

각 Chapter에서 배운 어휘와 구문, 문법을 복습, 확인하는 코너이다. 현장수업에서는 Weekly 테스트 또는 Daily 테스트로 활용하여 학습들의 실력과 복습 정도를 확인, 점검할 수 있다.

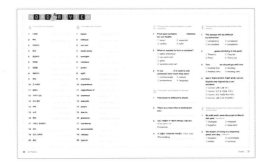

6 SENTENCE REVIEW

다양한 지문을 접한 후에 핵심 문법을 예문을 통해 다시 한 번 복습할 수 있게 한다. 간단한 문제를 통해 점검하되 제시된 문제는 수능어법 유형으로 확인 테스트를 할 수 있게 구성하였다.

7 Daily Assignment Book

그날의 시험내용과 과제물을 꼼꼼히 적어 학부형에게 확인 받아오는 시스템이다. 취약한 부분과 보완점을 스스로 작성해 보면서 자기 주도 학습이 가능하도록 만들었다.

8 WORKBOOK

CD 안의 무료 보충자료 워크북을 활용하여 Just Reading의 독해뿐 아니라, 어휘, 회화, 문법, 영작을 모두 최종 정리하며 복습할 수 있다. 본책에 해당하는 시험 적중률이 높은 유형의 문제들을 뽑았다. 숙제나 자습을 통해 보충하기에 탄탄한 자료이다.

C O N T E N T S

Prologue   4
About Reading   6
About Just Reading Series   9

Chapter 01   14

독해에 진짜 필요한 **Reading Skill** • 글의 순서   15
Unit **01** • 고래가 땅에서 살았다고요?   16
Unit **02** • 지문이 없어졌어요!   18
Unit **03** • 두껍아 새집 다오!   20
Unit **04** • 지상낙원 발견!   22
Unit **05** • 힘들 땐 한발 물러서기   24
WORD REVIEW   26
SENTENCE REVIEW   28

Chapter 02   30

독해에 진짜 필요한 **Reading Skill** • 내용 일치 여부 판단   31
Unit **01** • 맛을 봐야 아나요?   32
Unit **02** • 아무 이유 없이 우울해!   34
Unit **03** • 어느 길로 가야 하나요?   36
Unit **04** • 충고 새겨듣기   38
Unit **05** • 요거 안 먹히네!   40
WORD REVIEW   42
SENTENCE REVIEW   44

Chapter 03   46

독해에 진짜 필요한 **Reading Skill** • 무관한 문장 고르기   47
Unit **01** • 배우고 익힌 자   48
Unit **02** • 광고   50
Unit **03** • 자신의 일을 즐겨라!   52

Unit **04** ● 무위자연   54

Unit **05** ● 물에 뛰어드는 용기   56

WORD REVIEW   58

SENTENCE REVIEW   60

Chapter **04**   62

독해에 진짜 필요한 **Reading Skill** ● 빈칸 추론   63

Unit **01** ● 불교가 힌두교에 밀려?   64

Unit **02** ● 가장 한국적인 것   66

Unit **03** ● 할로윈   68

Unit **04** ● 신에 대한 도전   70

Unit **05** ● 테러의 고통과 슬픔   72

WORD REVIEW   74

SENTENCE REVIEW   76

Bonus Chapter ✚   80

독해에 진짜 필요한 **Reading Skill** ● 주어진 문장 넣기   81

Unit **01** ● 생각하는 대로!   82

Unit **02** ● 인어공주를 봤어요!   84

Unit **03** ● 하늘을 나는 포유류   86

Unit **04** ● 장군! 왜군이 옵니다!   88

Unit **05** ● 낮과 밤의 비밀   90

WORD REVIEW   92

SENTENCE REVIEW   94

WORD LIST   96

Answer Key   101

CD ● 해설집 + 워크북 + MP3 음성파일

Chapter

01

Unit 01 고래가 땅에서 살았다고요?

Unit 02 지문이 없어졌어요!

Unit 03 두껍아 새집 다오!

Unit 04 지상낙원 발견!

Unit 05 힘들 땐 한발 물러서기

 단원 어휘

- [ ] **huge** a. 거대한
- [ ] **surface** n. 표면, 수면
- [ ] **evolve** v. 진화하다
- [ ] **political** a. 정치(학)의
- [ ] **struggle** n. 싸움, 분쟁
- [ ] **a majority of** 대다수의
- [ ] **regardless of** ~와 관계없이
- [ ] **reflect** v. ~을 반영하다
- [ ] **fertile region** 비옥한 지역
- [ ] **available** a. 이용 가능한, 쓸모 있는
- [ ] **insulation** n. 단열재, 절연체
- [ ] **durability** n. 내구성, 내구력
- [ ] **access to** ~에 접근
- [ ] **fibrous** a. 섬유의, 섬유질의
- [ ] **ease** v. 진정시키다, 속도를 늦추다
- [ ] **altitude** n. 고도
- [ ] **orbit** n. 범위, 궤도
- [ ] **long for** v. 동경하다
- [ ] **irresistible** a. 억누를 수 없는
- [ ] **duration** n. 지속
- [ ] **attentive** a. 주의 깊은
- [ ] **land** v. 착륙하다

Mini Quiz Draw a line from each word on the left to its definition on the right. Then, use the numbered words to fill in the blanks in the sentences below.

1	huge	a.	the circular path of a planet, satellite, or moon
2	evolve	b.	to move safely down onto the ground
3	available	c.	to gradually develop over a period of time into something usually more advanced
4	orbit		
5	attentive	d.	able to be used or can easily be bought or found
6	land	e.	extremely large in size, amount, or degree
		f.	behaving toward somebody in a way that shows special regard or affection

7 It is believed that human beings _____ from apes.

8 This makes a(n) _____ difference, especially in the high school years.

9 The space shuttle is now in _____.

10 There are plenty of jobs _____ in this area.

11 Flight 846 _____ five minutes ago.

12 Customers want companies that are _____ to their needs.

글의 순서

글의 순서 문제는 주어진 문장에 이어질 문장들을 배열하여 문단의 구조와 문단의 통일성, 일관성, 응집성 등을 종합적으로 파악할 수 있는 능력을 평가하는 유형이다. 먼저 주어진 문장을 읽고, 글의 주제를 파악하고 나서, 이를 바탕으로 다음 글들이 어떻게 전개되어 나가야 하는지를 논리적으로 추론해 보는 것이 중요하다.

❶ **개략적인 글의 주제나 윤곽을 파악한다.** 주어진 문장을 먼저 읽고 이 글이 무엇에 관한 글이며, 작가가 어떤 식으로 글을 전개시킬지를 논리적으로 추론해 보는 것이 중요하다.

❷ **대명사와 지시어의 원관념을 파악한다.** 각 문장에 들어있는 지시어나 대명사, 반복어는 앞뒤에 있는 문장과의 관련성을 나타내는 중요한 단서가 되므로 적극적으로 활용해야 한다.

this, that, these, those, it, they, such, the + 명사	명사가 언급된 문장 뒤에 위치
대명사 they, he, she 등	성과 수가 일치하는 명사가 있는 문장 뒤에 위치
others(다른 사람들)	some 뒤에 위치
for these reasons	앞에 나온 원인들의 결론을 이끌 때(2개 이상의 이유를 구체적으로 제시)

❸ **연결사나 부사(구)를 활용한다.** 글의 흐름이 자연스럽게 전환될 수 있도록 문장을 이어주는 역할을 하는 연결어에 유의하여 문장 간의 연결 관계와 전후 관계를 찾는다.

대조	while, on the other hand, however, but, yet, still	앞의 내용은 상반된 내용
결과	therefore, thus, so, hence, as a result	앞의 내용은 이에 대한 원인
예시	for example, for instance	앞의 내용은 이를 포괄하는 내용
비교	likewise, similarly, in the same way, in like manner	앞의 내용은 유사한 내용
첨가	also, besides, furthermore, moreover, likewise, what is more, in addition	앞의 내용은 같은 내용
열거	to begin with, first, first of all, second, third, lastly, finally	앞의 내용은 이를 포괄하는 내용
기타	before, after, then, last	시간의 순서를 나타낸다.

주어진 문장 다음에 이어질 글의 순서로 가장 적절한 것은? 기출문제

We have the good fortune to live in a democracy.

(A) Without this freedom, the decision-makers may make our lives difficult because they wouldn't know what we think.

(B) We should, therefore, be ready to fight for the right to tell the truth whenever it is threatened.

(C) But what does democracy mean to us if we don't have the freedom to tell the truth?

① (A) - (B) - (C) ② (A) - (C) - (B) ③ (B) - (C) - (A)
④ (C) - (A) - (B) ⑤ (C) - (B) - (A)

[논리독해]

Key-word : democracy

(A) Without this freedom, ~
: (A)글 앞에는 자유가 언급되어 있어야 한다.

(B) We should, therefore, ~
: (B)글 앞에는 원인이 언급되어야 한다.

(C) But what does ~ ?
: 의문문 형식으로 논제를 제시하고 있다.

수험생의 눈

연결사나 대명사 등의 단서를 활용한다.

단락의 전개방식 – 의견 제시

Unit 01 고래가 땅에서 살았다고요?

Animal & Fact

A whale is a huge creature living in the ocean. A blue whale can grow up to 100 feet long, and a newborn blue whale is bigger than a full-grown elephant. There are many types of whales like the Sperm whale, Humpback whale, Sei Whale, Great blue whale, California Grey Whale, and Greenland Right Whale. A whale is a mammal because it is a warm-blooded animal, and the young are born out of their mother's womb and fed with the mother's milk. Since whales are mammals, they breathe through lungs, unlike fish that use gills for breathing. _____, whales must come up to the surface every half hour to breathe air. But isn't it strange that whales don't live on land like other mammals but live in water? According to zoologists, ancestors of whales used to live on land in very ancient times, but they evolved and became fishlike after they started living in water.

1 이 글의 내용과 일치하는 것은?

① Dolphins aren't part of the mammal family.
② Whales breathe through gills.
③ Whales must breathe air every hour or so.
④ All baby whales are born through their mother's womb.
⑤ Zoologists believe that whales were fishlike in ancient times.

2 **Choose the best word to fill in the blank.**

① Amazingly   ② Therefore   ③ In contrast
④ Likewise   ⑤ To begin with

Check Your VOCABULARY!

huge	full-grown	mammal	warm-blooded animal
womb	gill	surface	zoologist
ancestor	used to do	ancient	evolve

가주어 진주어 it ~ that 구문

🔽 **문장 맨 앞자리(주어 자리)**
[That people live longer than they did before] is true.
S는 ~~~~~~~~~~~~~~~~~~~~~~~~~~~~~~~~~~~~ 사실이다. (주어가 너무 길다.)

🔽 **It이 나오고 that**
It is true that people live longer than they did before.
사람들이 예전보다 더 오래 산다는 것은 사실이다.

주어가 길어지면 그 자리에 it을 쓰고 모두 뒤로 보낼 수 있다고 했다. 주어 자리에 명사절 접속사 that이 오면 주어는 정말로 길어질 수 있다. 이때도 주어 자리에 마찬가지로 it을 쓰고 모두 뒤로 보내는데, 이를 가주어(it), 진주어(that)라 한다.

사람들이 더 오래 산다 + ~(는)것
➡ 사람들이 더 오래 산다는 것

people live longer + **that**
➡ **that** people live longer~

우리말은 단어 자체를 바꿔 말을 만든다. 영어는 that이 '주어 + 동사'를 데리고 있는 덩어리가 문장 맨 앞자리에 오거나 It을 쓰고 뒤로 that이 이끄는 문장이 있을 때 that 안의 동사를 우리말 '~(는) 것(을), ~라고'의 의미를 나타내는데 정해진 그 자리에서만 뜻을 나타낼 수 있다.

Practice

1 It is very surprising that many of the most educated people in our society know so little of our country's history.

해석 ◑ _____

2 신이 God 천지를 the whole world 창조했다는 것은 created 확실하지 않다 not clear.

영작 ◑ _____

Super Speaking

1단계 : 처음 우리말과 영문을 보면서 영어로 말해본다.
2단계 : 영문을 손으로 가리고 우리말만 보면서 완전한 영어로 말할 수 있도록 3~4회 반복한다.

 사람들이 늘 휴일을 갖고 싶어 하는 것은 당연하다.

It is natural that people always want to have holidays.
우리말을 영어로 옮기기

 침대에서 독서하는 것은 나쁜 버릇이다.

It is a bad habit that people read in bed.

 그녀가 내 이름을 기억하지 못했던 것은 이상한 일이었다.

It was strange that she didn't remember my name.

 우리가 다른 에너지 원천을 찾아야 한다는 것은 분명하다.

It is clear that we should find another source of energy.

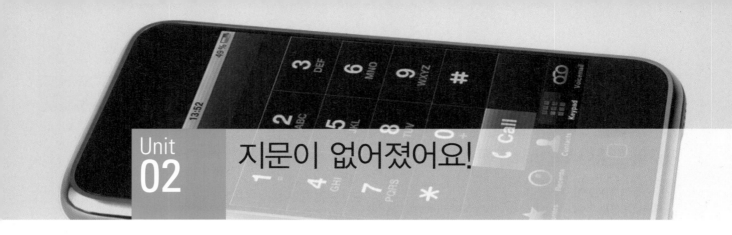

Unit 02 지문이 없어졌어요!

Issue & Society

According to a recent survey, at least five out of ten Korean people are mobile phone users. Mobile phones can be used to solve conflicts. In a recent political struggle between politicians and prosecutors, the two sides were able to solve their problems over mobile phones. However, the mobile phone may also cause a lot of problems. A majority of car-related accidents these days are caused by people who talk on the phone while driving, or crossing a busy street. In Korea, it is very common to see old people as well as children talking on their mobile phones regardless of time or place. The ring tones of mobile phones are often terribly sharp and annoying. Even if the phone has a musical ring tone, it is still disturbingly noisy. When it rings in a movie theater, or in a concert hall, the lousy ringing sounds disturb and annoy the public. Those problems caused by mobile phones reflect the endless needs of Korean people to be connected with others.

1   **According to the passage, what is a disadvantage of the mobile phone use?**

① Children talk on their mobile phones instead of studying.

② Mobile phones can cause brain cancer.

③ Mobile phones can cause car accidents.

④ It is difficult to talk to somebody when you can't see his or her face.

⑤ Mobile phones cause a lot of diseases.

2   **Why are mobile phones popular in Korea?**

① Korean people have endless reasons to be connected with others.

② People like to talk to their friends when they are stuck in traffic.

③ Mobile phones are not very expensive.

④ There are few public phones in Korea.

⑤ They are important in case of an emergency.

Check Your VOCABULARY!

conflict	political	struggle	politician
prosecutor	a majority of	regardless of	annoying
disturbingly	lousy	disturb	reflect

구문으로 익히는 **Writing & Speaking**

가주어 진주어 it ~ to 구문

⬇ It이 나오고 to v   ⬇ It이 나오고 to v
It is important for a journalist to be honorable and to write about both sides of a problem.
언론인이 명예를 지키고 문제의 양 측면에 대해서 글을 쓰는 것은 중요하다.

Because women were physically weaker than men, the knights
⬇ It이 나오고 to v
believed that it was their duty to protect them.
여자들은 신체적으로 남자보다 더 약했기 때문에, 기사들은 여자들을 보호하는 것이 자기들의 의무라고 믿었다.

영어는 주어와 동사를 가급적 가까이 위치해야 말을 빨리 전달할 수 있다. 그래서 주어가 조금이라도 길어지면 그 자리에 'it'을 쓰고 전부 뒤로 보낼 수 있다. 주어가 To부정사로 시작되면 어쩔 수 없이 길어질 수밖에 없다. 이 때 현대 영어에서는 가급적 It을 그 자리에 두고 모두 뒤로 보내버린다.

보호하다 + ~(는) 것 ➡ 보호하는 것
protect + to ➡ to protect

우리말은 단어 자체를 바꿔 말을 만드는 말이다. 영어는 그런 장치가 없어서 동사 앞에 to를 붙여 정해진 자리에 들어가야지만 그 뜻을 나타낼 수 있다. to부정사는 문장 맨 앞자리와 동사 바로 뒷자리에 있을 때 '~(는) 것(을), ~기'의 뜻을 갖는다. 원래 문장 맨 앞자리에 있던 to부정사가 it을 쓰고 보낸 것이므로 it이 나오고 to부정사가 나오면 우리말 '~(는)것, ~기'로 해석된다.

Practice

1 Because the student has short legs and is not strong, it is difficult for him to be an excellent soccer player. As a result, he is learning golf and table tennis.

해석 ◐ _____

2 아이들에게 children 그들이 원하는 모든 것을 everything they want 주는 것은 to give 잘못이다 wrong.

영작 ◐ _____

Super Speaking
1단계 : 처음 우리말과 영문을 보면서 영어로 말해본다.
2단계 : 영문을 손으로 가리고 우리말만 보면서 완전한 영어로 말할 수 있도록 3~4회 반복한다.

  요즈음 스마트폰 없이 사는 것은 어렵다.

It is difficult to live without a smartphone nowadays. 우리말을 영어로 옮기기

  로마를 여행하는 동안 우리가 보기를 희망했던 경치를 보는 것은 어려웠다.
During our trip to Rome, it was difficult to see all the sights that we had hoped to see.

  성형수술을 하는 것은 시간과 돈 낭비이다.
It is a waste of time and money to have plastic surgery.

두껍아 새집 다오!

Reason

Around the world, the ways to construct a house usually depend on the _____ of building materials. For instance, people who live in fertile regions use the most available materials, mud or clay, which block out the heat and solar radiation. They also provide good insulation and durability from the heat. On the other hand, the Eskimos, living in some parts of the Arctic, build their houses with thick blocks of ice because they live in a treeless region of snow and ice. In Northern Europe, Russia, and other areas of the world where people have easy access to forests, houses are usually made of wood. Also, in the islands of the South Pacific, there grow bamboos and palm trees. So, people use these tough, fibrous plants to build their houses.

1   **Choose the best word to fill in the blank.**

① size   ② availability   ③ price   ④ demand   ⑤ kinds

2   이 글의 내용을 다음 한 문장으로 요약하고자 한다. 빈칸 (A)와 (B)에 들어갈 말로 가장 적절한 것끼리 짝지은 것은?

> The paragraph shows that people are _____(A)_____ enough to adapt to their environment because they have been _____(B)_____ in various environments throughout history.

	(A)		(B)
①	idle	...	hard working
②	noxious	...	constructing
③	intelligent	...	surviving
④	foolish	...	creating
⑤	calm	...	engaging

Check Your
VOCABULARY!

fertile region	available	block	solar radiation
insulation	durability	Arctic	access to
be made of	bamboo	palm tree	fibrous

명사 바로 뒷자리에 줄을 서는 관계사 who

🔽 **명사 뒷자리**
The child who doesn't make the baseball team feels terrible.
야구팀에 합류하지 못한 그 아이는 기분이 몹시 좋지 않다.
🔽 **명사 뒷자리**
I saw the musician who electrified the audience on TV last night.
나는 지난밤에 TV에서 청중을 전율시킨 음악가를 보았어.

관계대명사가 선행사를 수식하는 경우는 어떨 때 가능한가? 관계사의 역할을 하려면 who 또는 which, that도 모두 똑같이 반드시 명사 바로 뒷자리에 위치해야 한다. 이 때의 관계사절 안의 동사가 우리말 '~하는, ~했던, ~할, ~ㄴ(니은)'의 뜻을 나타내어 앞에 있는 명사를 꾸며준다. who, which, that은 특별한 의미나 해석을 갖지 않는 기능적인 역할만을 하게 된다. 어법에서는 주어를 수식하는 경우에 동사의 '수일치'와, '시제일치'에 대해 자주 물어보게 된다.

전율시키다 + ~하는(했던) ➡ 전율시키는
electrified + **who** ➡ **who** electrified

우리말은 명사를 꾸미는 말은 형용사를 기본으로 그 어떤 말이든 명사 앞에서 꾸민다. 우리말은 단어에 형용사 어미 'ㄴ(니은)'을 만들어 명사를 꾸미지만 영어는 who를 명사 바로 뒷자리에 두어 '~하는, 했던, ㄴ(니은)'의 역할을 자리로 나타낼 수 있다.

Practice

1 They look for employees who support each other, take pride in their work, and encourage maintenance of a pleasant working environment.

해석 ◐ _____

2 자신에게 in himself 신뢰를 갖고 있는 has faith 사람이 a person 다른 사람들에게 충실할 수 있다 can be faithful to others.

영작 ◐ _____

Super Speaking

1단계 : 처음 우리말과 영문을 보면서 영어로 말해본다.
2단계 : 영문을 손으로 가리고 우리말만 보면서 완전한 영어로 말할 수 있도록 3~4회 반복한다.

 사업이나 직업에서 성공하지 못하는 사람들은 집중력이 부족한 사람들이다.

Those who cannot achieve success in their business or profession are the ones whose concentration is poor.

 우리말을 영어로 옮기기

 내 친구 피터는 내가 신뢰할 수 있는 사람이다.

My friend Peter is a person who I can trust.

 도시에 사는 대부분의 사람들이 대중교통 수단을 이용해서 다닌다.

Most people who live in cities get around using public transportation.

 우리가 이번 여름에 봤던 영화들은 모두 좋았다.

The movies which we watched this summer were all good.

Adventure

(A)

"**There** is a good reason to make this trip to the Island of Paradise," Captain Koppe told himself as he stepped out of the elevator car into (i) the covered rooftop hangar of his house. The journey itself would be of use. There were times (ii) when it was important to be alone, to have time to think. Alone even from one's personal robot, from one's trusted wife.

(B)

The outer doors opened, and the aircar slowly eased out into the driving rain. Suddenly, (a) it was in the middle of the storm, jumping and swinging in the darkness, the rain crashing down on the windows with incredible violence. The storm boomed and roared outside the long-range aircar as (b) it fought for altitude, the banging and clattering (iii) getting worse with every moment.

(C)

Smooth sailing after the storm, the aircar arrived at the orbit of the Island of Paradise. Captain Koppe looked out at the island through the window. He had been longing for (c) it since his childhood. At that moment, his family picture (iv) posted on the inside of the aircar came into his eyes. All of a sudden, he had an irresistible urge to go to see his beloved wife and his two sons. He turned his back on the Island of Paradise and directed (d) it toward the homeland.

(D)

Captain Koppe sensed that this was one of those times when he had to be alone – if for no other reason than to remind himself that he (v) should have to make his decision alone. And he would have the duration of the flight all to himself. The thought appealed to him as he powered up the aircar and (e) it lifted a half-meter or so off the deck of the hangar. 기출

*hangar 격납고

1 글 (A)에 이어질 내용을 순서에 맞게 배열한 것으로 가장 적절한 것은?

① (B) − (C) − (D)

② (C) − (B) − (D)

③ (C) − (D) − (B)

④ (D) − (B) − (C)

⑤ (D) − (C) − (B)

2 이 글의 내용과 일치하는 것은?

① 비행선에는 로봇 승무원들도 탑승하였다.

② 비행선이 낙원의 섬에 비상 착륙했다.

③ Koppe 선장은 낙원의 섬에서 친구를 만났다.

④ Koppe 선장은 가족이 몹시 보고 싶어졌다.

⑤ Koppe 선장은 우주 비행단과 함께 여행했다.

3 밑줄 친 (a)~(e) 중에서 가리키는 대상이 나머지 넷과 다른 것은?

① (a)   ② (b)   ③ (c)

④ (d)   ⑤ (e)

4 밑줄 친 (i)~(v) 중에서 어법상 어색한 것은?

① (i)   ② (ii)   ③ (iii)

④ (iv)   ⑤ (v)

Check Your
VOCABULARY!

rooftop

of use

aircar

ease

swing

crash

incredible

violence

boom

roar

long-range

altitude

bang

clatter

smooth

orbit

long for

all of a sudden

irresistible

urge

duration

appeal to

power up

lift

deck

힘들 땐 한발 물러서기

Moral

(A)

Usually it is important not to stick to _____ . (a) Especially in a hospital when emergency situations happen, Dr. Neal Flomenbaum says, team leaders are required not to be overly attentive to medical procedures, but to find the best ways to handle the situation and supervise others. (b) Also, they should ignore other emergency patients because there are many other doctors available to take care of them. (c) "It's important to have someone who stands back and keeps the whole situation under control," he says. (d) "Otherwise a patient's life can be at risk." (e) My friend Schorn, an Aloha pilot, once told me, "When you land a plane, the most important thing is to remember what your priority is. It is landing."

(B)

Sometimes, we struggle over _____ at the cost of larger objectives. In order not to make a mistake of losing the whole forest while saving one tree, we should keep asking ourselves whether the details we are working on fit into the larger picture or not. If they don't, we should stop and move on to something else. For example, the Apollo 11 mission couldn't have been possible if the astronauts had lost sight of the big picture. When the spacecraft was coming back to Earth, it was not exactly following its route. However, it could successfully land on the ground because the astronauts knew exactly where they were headed. Therefore, they could make the necessary adjustments instead of changing the whole route. There is no difference in daily life: knowing what we want to achieve in our lives helps us judge the importance of every task we undertake.

1 글 (A)와 (B)의 빈칸에 공통으로 들어가기에 가장 적절한 것은?

① details
② aims
③ results
④ plans
⑤ directions

2 글 (A)와 (B)가 공통으로 시사하는 바로 가장 적절한 것은?

① We should not overlook details.
② We should keep our composure in emergency situations.
③ Your sincere efforts will be paid off sooner or later.
④ Teamwork is very important when you perform a difficult task.
⑤ We should be able to see the bigger picture.

3 글 (A)와 (B)에 대한 설명으로 일치하지 <u>않는</u> 것은?

① In (A), all doctors must always be very meticulous in medical procedures.
② In (A), it is significant for a leader to manage the situation.
③ In (B), it is suggested that we should always look ahead.
④ In (B), the Apollo 11 mission was successful.
⑤ In (B), it is important to know what we want to accomplish in our lives.

4 글 (A)에서 전체 흐름과 관계 <u>없는</u> 문장은?

① (a)
② (b)
③ (c)
④ (d)
⑤ (e)

stick to

emergency situation

overly

attentive

procedure

supervise

ignore

under control

otherwise

at risk

land

priority

struggle

cost

objective

in order to

fit (into)

lose sight of

exactly

route

adjustment

achieve

judge

undertake

overlook

composure

meticulous

WORD REVIEW

A Translate into English.

1 거대한

2 고대의

3 동물학자

4 조상

5 갈등, 분쟁

6 정치(학)의

7 정치인

8 검사, 검찰관

9 막다, 차단하다

10 북극

11 섬유의, 섬유가 많은

12 내구성(력)

13 비행선

14 범위, 궤도

15 고도

16 동경하다

17 ~를 고수하다, 얽매이다

18 감독 하에, 지시 하에

19 감독하다, 관리하다

20 ~에 적합하다

21 진화하다

22 짜증나게 하는

23 비옥한 지역

24 이용 가능한

25 (일을) 맡다, 책임지다

B Translate into Korean.

1 surface

2 used to do

3 mammal

4 gill

5 a majority of

6 regardless of

7 struggle

8 reflect

9 insulation

10 palm tree

11 access to

12 solar radiation

13 clatter

14 duration

15 incredible

16 of use

17 adjustment

18 ease

19 land

20 procedure

21 disturbingly

22 irresistible

23 urge

24 attentive

25 objective

C Choose the correct answers to each question.

1 The ancestors of whales used to live on land in ancient times, but they _____ and became fishlike.

① involved   ② evolved

③ breathed   ④ supervised

2 Eskimos, living in some parts of the Arctic, build their houses with thick _____ of ice.

① bamboos   ② palm trees

③ block   ④ blocks

3 A whale is a _____ because it is a warm-blooded animal, and the young are born out of their mothers' womb and fed with their mothers' milk.

① ancestor   ② cold-blooded animal

③ mammal   ④ fishlike

D Translate into English or Korean.

1 It was shocking that nobody stood up and helped the old woman.

_____

2 He predicted not only that war would break out in 2010 but also who would win.

_____

3 이 게임의 법칙은 사람들이 질문을 하면 그 대답을 아는 사람들이 그것을 설명하는 것이다. (people, questions, other people, who, explain)

The rule of this game is that _____ _____ and then _____ _____ .

E Choose the correct words to fill in the blanks.

1 _____ is very surprising that people on the beach fed fish and the fish came up to the beach.

① What   ② That   ③ Which   ④ It

2 A doctor advised _____ she should not get up.

① that   ② and   ③ so   ④ it

3 Those people _____ were severely injured in the accident were carried to the emergency room.

① why   ② who   ③ where   ④ what

4 These are the products _____ were made in China and should be refunded right away.

① where   ② who   ③ which   ④ what

F Match each word with its synonyms. (two answers)

1 huge

2 material

3 durability

4 orbit

5 achieve

a. stuff

b. course

c. endurance

d. magnificent

e. accomplish

f. resources

g. fulfill

h. enormous

i. sturdiness

j. path

★ 의미상 목적어가 필요 없는 자동사 occur, appear, seem, remain, happen 등은 수동태로 쓸 수 없다.

Researchers said the maximum number of all eclipses that can **occur** in a year is five.

연구원들이 말하길 일 년에 일어날 수 있는 최대의 일식 수는 5번이라고 했다.

People often find their dreams **remain** unaccomplished and give up.

사람들은 종종 자신들의 꿈이 이뤄지지 않은 채로 있는 것을 발견하고 포기한다.

★ 수동태에서 by 대신 다른 전치사를 사용하는 경우를 주의해야 한다.

be covered **with** / be filled **with** / be made **of** / be satisfied **with** / be disappointed **in** / be surprised **at** ...

Terrorists will use anything that they can cause people to *be scared* **of** something actual or fictional.

테러리스트는 실제 사실 또는 허구적인 일로 사람들을 무서워하게 만들기 위해 어떤 것이든 사용할 것이다.

★ 비교문에서 비교대상은 어법상 동일 어구를 사용해야 한다.

My family *prefers* **eating** outside *to* **eating** at home on special occasions like Christmas.

크리스마스 같은 특별한 때에 우리 가족은 집에서 먹는 것보다 외식하는 것을 더 좋아한다.

To evaluate each student is more effective than **to evaluate** the group of students.

학생 개개인을 평가하는 것은 학생들 그룹을 평가하는 것보다 더 효과적이다.

1 다음 괄호 안에서 알맞은 것을 고르시오.

When you send an e-mail to your friend, your nickname will [appear / be appeared] in the "From" field.

2 다음 문장에서 틀린 부분을 찾아 바르게 고치시오.

I remember being surprised on how good the pictures we had taken actually came out.
　　　①　　　②　　　　③　　　　　　　　　　　④

➡ _____

3 다음 문장에서 틀린 부분을 찾아 바르게 고치시오.

How you see yourself is different from others see you when you talk with people.

➡ _____

Homeroom teacher : _____

수업일	Contents (수업내용)	Homework (과제물)	Check (숙제검사)	
월 일			Done	Didn't do
월 일			Done	Didn't do
월 일			Done	Didn't do
나의 학습 아킬레스건	나의 취약 부분은?		Done	Didn't do
	해결 방법은?		Done	Didn't do
		Parent's Signature		

※ 학생들이 학원에서 공부한 내용입니다. 바쁘시더라도 관심을 갖고 확인해 주십시오.

청량음료 브랜드

청량음료의 브랜드. 북미에서는 캐드베리-스웝스 아메리카스 베버리지스(Cadbury Schweppes Americas Beverages: 줄여서 CSAB)가, 그 외의 나라에서는 펩시코(PepsiCo)가 소유하고 있습니다. 1920년에 미국인 찰스 그리그(Charles L. Grigg)가 세인트루이스에 청량음료 회사 '하우디 코퍼레이션 (Howdy Corporation)'을 설립했습니다. 그는 1929년 10월 월스트리트 주가대폭락이 있기 2주 전에 레몬라임 맛의 탄산음료 '빕-라벨 리티에이티드 레몬-라임 소다(Bib-Label Lithiated Lemon-Lime Soda)'를 출시했죠. 당시 미국의 청량음료 시장은 코카콜라가 장악하고 있었고, 600 종류가 넘는 레몬라임 맛 음료가 나와 있었어요. 그러나 카페인이 없고 조울증 치료제로 쓰이는 구연산 리튬(lithium citrate)을 함유한 이 신제품은 건강음료로 부각되어 경제적으로 어려운 시기에도 크게 성공할 수 있었습니다.

브랜드명은 후에 '세븐업 리티에이티드 레몬소다(7Up Lithiated Lemon Soda)'를 거쳐 1936년에 '세븐업(7Up)'으로 변경되었고, 같은 해에 회사명도 '세븐업 컴퍼니(Seven Up Company)'로 변경되었습니다. 세븐업이란 브랜드명의 유래는 정확히 알려져 있지 않으나 제품에 들어간 성분 7가지와 탄산방울이 위로 올라오는(up) 모습에서 유래되었다는 설, 초기 제품의 7온스짜리 포장 용기에서 유래되었다는 설, 7음절로 이루어진 초기 제품의 이름에서 유래되었다는 설 등이 있죠. 1961년에 경쟁사 코카콜라 회사는 세븐업과 비슷한 '스프라이트(Sprite)'를 출시했으나 1980년 이전까지는 세븐업의 아성을 무너뜨리지 못했습니다. 2000년에 세븐업 브랜드 마스코트 '피도 디도(Fido Dido)'를 만들었습니다. 2006년에 고과당 콘시럽(HFCS)으로 단맛을 내고 구연 산나트륨을 첨가한 100% 천연성분의 신제품을 출시했습니다.

1978년 6월에 필립 모리스(Philip Morris)가 세븐업 컴퍼니를 인수했습니다. 1986년에 개인투자그룹(Private Investment Group)이 필립 모리스로부터 세븐업을 인수했어요. 그리고 닥터페퍼 컴퍼니(Dr Pepper Company)와 세븐업을 합병하여 텍사스 주의 댈러스에 본사를 둔 '닥터페퍼/세븐업(Dr Pepper/Seven Up, Inc.: 줄여서 DPSU)'을 설립했죠. 두 회사의 합병 후 세븐업의 북미 지역 이외에서의 판매권은 펩시코가, 닥터 페퍼의 북미 지역 이외에서의 판매권은 코카콜라가 인수했습니다. 1995년에 영국의 제과, 음료 회사인 '캐드베리-스웝스 아메리카스 베버리지스'가 닥터페퍼/세븐업을 인수하여 세븐업과 닥터페퍼의 북미 판매권을 소유하게 되었습니다.

Chapter 02

Unit 01 맛을 봐야 아나요?

Unit 02 아무 이유 없이 우울해!

Unit 03 어느 길로 가야 하나요?

Unit 04 충고 새겨듣기

Unit 05 요거 안 먹히네!

단원 어휘

- ☐ detergent n. 세정제, 세제
- ☐ advertise v. 광고하다, 선전하다
- ☐ depressed a. 우울한
- ☐ lighten v. 기운 나게 하다
- ☐ be willing to 기꺼이 ~하다
- ☐ pronunciation n. 발음
- ☐ consonant n. 자음 a. 자음의
- ☐ articulate v. 또렷하게 발음하다
- ☐ vocabulary n. 단어, 어휘
- ☐ tempt v. 유혹하다, 마음을 끌다
- ☐ fame n. 명성, 평판
- ☐ acknowledged a. 인정받은
- ☐ master v. 숙달하다
- ☐ frequently adv. 자주, 여러 번
- ☐ ignore v. 무시하다
- ☐ gradually adv. 점진적으로
- ☐ regret v. 후회하다
- ☐ screw up 망치다, 엉망으로 만들다
- ☐ pretend v. ~인 체하다
- ☐ deceive v. 속이다
- ☐ expression n. 표정
- ☐ appetite n. 식욕

Mini Quiz

Draw a line from each word on the left to its definition on the right. Then, use the numbered words to fill in the blanks in the sentences below.

1 detergent

2 lighten

3 vocabulary

4 regret

5 pretend

6 expression

a. to feel sorry about something you have done and wish you had not done it

b. to make you feel more cheerful, happy, and relaxed

c. a look on someone's face that shows what they are thinking or feeling

d. a liquid or powder used for washing clothes, dishes, etc

e. all the words that someone knows or uses

f. to behave as if something is true when in fact you know it is not, in order to deceive people or for fun

7 Are you sure it's all right to wash this skirt with regular _____?

8 Let's _____ we're on the moon.

9 He _____ having eaten so much at the party.

10 Reading is one of the best ways of improving your _____.

11 There was a blank _____ on her face.

12 He tried to _____ up those who were upset.

독해에 진짜 필요한 **Reading Skill**

내용 일치 여부 판단

주어진 글에서 제시되는 구체적 정보를 정확히 파악할 수 있는 독해 능력을 측정하는 유형으로 주로 특정한 인물의 인생 여정이나 경험담, 그리고 특정한 사물이나 동물의 특징 등과 관련된 글의 일치 여부를 가릴 수 있도록 선택지를 구성하여 제시한다. 핵심어나 글의 전개방식 등을 파악하여 주제를 중심으로 추론해가는 다른 유형들과는 달리 사실적인 이해여부를 묻고 있으므로 선택지의 내용을 미리 읽은 후 본문을 읽으면서 관련 내용에 밑줄을 긋고 선택지와 서로 비교하면서 일치 또는 불일치의 여부를 파악하는 것이 좋다.

내용일치 유형의 급소	❶ **문제와 선택지를 보면 핵심어와 글의 내용이 보인다.** 문제와 선택지부터 반드시 확인하여 본문의 내용이 무엇에 관한 글인지 예상한다. 가령, 문제가 '태양열 비행기에 관한 다음 글의 내용과 일치하지 않는 것은?'이라면 글의 핵심어가 '태양열 비행기'임을 알 수 있고, 또한 선택지의 내용들은 본문의 어휘와 내용으로 만들기 때문에 선택지의 내용을 영어로 바꾸어 생각할 수 있는 부분을 생각하면서 글을 읽는다. ❷ **꼼꼼하게 읽으며 내용 일치 여부를 확인한다.** 이미 머릿속에 정리된 선택지의 내용과 자신이 읽은 본문에 관련된 단어와 어구를 맞춰 보면서 내용을 하나씩 소거해 나가는 방법을 이용한다. ❸ **본문에 제시된 정보만을 근거로 답을 찾는다.** 알고 있는 상식이나 내용을 유추해서 답을 고르지 말고 본문에서 언급된 내용에 따라 답을 찾아야 한다. 선택지의 내용이 글의 내용을 유추해서 제시된 경우도 있으므로 글의 내용을 통해 알 수 있는 사실을 추론해야 하는 경우 지나친 비약을 지양하고 객관적인 증거 자료에 의해 추론한다. ❹ **정답은 주로 중반 이후에 나온다.** 보통 선택지는 본문에 나오는 어휘나 내용을 가지고 만들어 낸다. 주의할 것은 본문의 내용과 달리, 선택지에서는 주체와 대상을 바꿔 제시하여 함정을 유도할 수 있다는 점이다. 예를 들어 '미국과 달리 콜롬비아 정부는 커피 재배를 장려하고 있다.'라는 내용인데, 선택지에서는 '② 미국과 마찬가지로 콜롬비아 정부는 커피 재배를 장려하고 있다.'라는 식으로 주체만 달리하여 함정을 만들어 놓는다는 것이다.

Anita에 관한 설명 중, 다음 글의 내용과 일치하는 것은? 기출문제

[1] Never in good health as a child, Anita lost her hearing at ten. [2] Her father's business failed while she was in high school, so she quit school and found a job as [3] a nurse's assistant in a hospital for homeless people. Here Anita became interested in social welfare. [4] At night she attended classes in composition and developed her writing skills. Soon she was writing newspaper articles. [5] By thirty-five she had established herself as a writer. Although her life was difficult, she never gave up. In her nineties, she said in an interview, "Life is a wonderful teacher if we only listen to its lessons."

① 성인이 되어서 청각을 상실했다.
② 대학 재학 중 아버지가 사업에 실패했다.
③ 병원에서 간호보조원으로 일했다.
④ 야간 학교 교사로 근무했다.
⑤ 40세가 지나서 작가가 되었다.

[논리독해]

Key-word : Anita의 인생 여정

1 lost her hearing at ten
  열 살 때 청력을 잃음
2 ~ failed ~ in high school
  고등학교 때 사업 실패
3 간호보조원으로 일했다(O)
4 At night she attended classes ~
  야간에 수업을 들었다.
5 By thirty-five she ~ as a writer
  35세에 작가로 자리를 잡았다.

단락의 전개방식

▶ Time order
  (시간의 순서에 의한 나열)

Unit 01 맛을 봐야 아나요?

Episode

One day, Jason found a small yellow bottle in his mailbox. On the label of the bottle, there was a picture of two lemons with the words "with Fresh Lemon Juice." "Awesome!" said Jason. "This is a free sample of lemon dressing! I guess I should have a salad for dinner. Hopefully, the salad will taste good with this lemon dressing." Jason put the contents of the yellow bottle on his salad. That night, he had a stomachache. As a matter of fact, the bottle was a free sample from a soap company. The soap company mailed their new liquid dish detergent to millions of people. It said "with Fresh Lemon Juice" on the label, because the company wanted to advertise that the detergent had a good smell. However, Jason was not the only person who read the label wrong. A lot of people thought it was lemon dressing. So they put the soap on dishes or on salads. Later they felt sick, too. Most of the people had stomachaches; but got over their illnesses in a few hours. Luckily, no one died from eating the soap.

1   **What can you learn from this paragraph?**
   ① Strike the iron while it is hot.
   ② Nothing ventured, nothing gained.
   ③ Look before you leap.
   ④ The early bird catches the worm.
   ⑤ Don't put the cart before the horse.

2   이 글의 주인공 Jason의 심경 변화로 가장 적절한 것은?

   ① delighted → regretful   ② unhappy → excited
   ③ unexpected → ecstatic   ④ curious → calm
   ⑤ astonished → satisfied

Check Your VOCABULARY!

mailbox	label	awesome	hopefully
content	stomachache	as a matter of fact	soap
liquid	detergent	advertise	get over

구문으로 익히는 Writing & Speaking

동사 바로 뒤에 있는 명사절 접속사 that 생략

⬇ 주어 　　 ⬇ 동사 　　 ⬇ 주어 　　 ⬇ 동사
The bank did not realize the clerk had been stealing money.
그 은행은 그 직원이 돈을 훔쳐 왔다는 것을 알아차리지 못했다.

⬇ 주어 　 ⬇ 동사 　 ⬇ 주어 　 ⬇ 동사
I at first thought the house was on fire. But as I turned the corner, I realized the whole house was shining with light.
나는 처음에 집에 불이 났다고 생각했다. 그러나 모퉁이를 돌아서자, 집 전체가 햇살로 빛나고 있음을 알아차렸다.

명사절의 생략은 어떨 때 가능한가? 글을 읽다가 '주어 + 동사 + (that 생략) + 주어 + 동사' 즉, '주동 주동'이 연이어 나오는 경우, 동사와 바로 뒷자리에 있는 주어 사이에 명사절 접속사 that이 생략되어 있다고 보면 된다. 영어는 정해진 자리에서만 그 뜻이 결정되므로 동사 뒷자리에 나오는 주어, 동사를 해석해서 우리말 '~것(을), ~라고, ~다고'로 해석한다.

그 집에 불이 났다 + ~다(라)고
➡ 그 집에 불이 났다(라)고
the house was on fire + that
➡ that the house was on fire

that이 이끄는 문장이 동사 바로 뒷자리에 있을 때만 우리말 '것(을), ~라(다)고'의 뜻을 나타낸다. 이때 that을 생략해서 쓰므로 동사 바로 뒷자리에 주어(명사)와 동사가 연이어 나오게 된다.

Practice

1 Many scientists believe the earth was created by something.

해석 ◐ _____

2 대부분의 대학생들은 most college students 좋은 직업을 good jobs 찾기가 어렵다는 hard to find 것을 안다 know.

영작 ◐ _____

Super Speaking

1단계 : 처음 우리말과 영문을 보면서 영어로 말해본다.
2단계 : 영문을 손으로 가리고 우리말만 보면서 완전한 영어로 말할 수 있도록 3~4회 반복한다.

 그녀는 이와 같은 기회가 다시 없을 것이라는 것을 알고 있다.

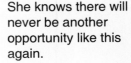 She knows there will never be another opportunity like this again.

 우리말을 영어로 옮기기

 아이들조차도 지구가 둥글다는 것을 안다.

Even children know the earth is round.

 우리들은 부모님이 우리를 항상 사랑한다는 것을 안다.

We know our parents always love us.

 대부분의 사람들은 비틀즈가 최고의 락 밴드라고 생각한다.

Most people think the Beatles is the best rock band.

아무 이유 없이 우울해!

Psychology

The changes of weather seem to have an influence on our _____. Some people feel gloomy when the sky gets dark, and some people even feel depressed during the rainy season. It seems like rain or dark clouds make people sad and depressed for no reason. People may have these negative feelings, because they have to stay indoors too long during bad weather. In contrast, a sunny day can lighten one's mood. Most of us would agree that the sunshine makes us energetic and happy. When the weather is pleasant, people tend to be friendlier and more willing to help each other. For example, one study found that waiters and waitresses receive bigger tips on sunny days. The most interesting fact that weather affects our mood is the relationship between how much one stays outside and what season it is. Some people are big summer fans because summer has more daylight and sunshine.

1   **Choose the best word to fill in the blank.**

① job   ② mood   ③ health
④ fashion   ⑤ lifestyle

2   이 글에서 글쓴이가 주장하는 바로 가장 알맞은 것은?

① All the people feel more cheerful on fine days.
② Many people's lives depend on the weather.
③ Weather can treat people's mental states.
④ Weather has a big effect on our everyday lives.
⑤ Some people become depressed in the rainy seasons.

Check Your
VOCABULARY!

seem	influence	gloomy	depressed
negative feeling	indoors	in contrast	lighten
tend to do	friendly	be willing to	affect

구문으로 익히는 **Writing & Speaking**

동격의 that절

⬇ 명사 fact 뒷자리
The fact that *he is honest* is clear.
그가 정직하다는 사실은 분명하다.

⬇ 명사 news 뒷자리
The news that *his son was killed* is false.
그의 아들이 살해당했다는 소식은 거짓이다.

특정명사(fact, belief, truth, news, rumor, idea, opinion 등)가 명사절 앞에 올 때, 동격절이 되는 경우가 있다. the fact 뒤에는 현대영어에서 'that'만을 사용한다. 관계사절과 똑같이 해석해도 무관하나, 앞에 있는 명사를 꾸미면서 우리말 '~라는, ~다는'으로 해석하면 된다.

그의 아들이 살해당했다 + ~라(다)는
➡ 그의 아들이 살해당했**다라는**
his son was killed + **that**
➡ **that** his son was killed

우리말 '~라는, ~다는' 말을 표현하려면 영어는 정해진 자리에 들어가야 한다. the fact와 같이 특정명사 바로 뒷자리에 that이 있으면 그 자리가 바로 '~라는'의 의미값을 갖는다. 우리말도 명사 앞에서 꾸미는 말을 'ㄴ(니은)'으로 고치듯이 영어도 명사 바로 뒷자리에 있는 모든 말은 'ㄴ(니은)'의 형용사 어미가 되어 앞에 있는 명사를 꾸며준다.

Practice

1 Research confirms the popular wisdom that age is more a state of mind than of body.

해석 ◐ _____

2 그 노인은 the old man 자신이 여전히 살아 있다는 he was still alive 그 사실에 대해 for the fact that 항상 신에게 감사했다 always thanked God.

영작 ◐ _____

Super Speaking

1단계 : 처음 우리말과 영문을 보면서 영어로 말해본다.
2단계 : 영문을 손으로 가리고 우리말만 보면서 완전한 영어로 말할 수 있도록 3~4회 반복한다.

 현재 우리의 스트레스는 시간이 충분치 않다라는 우리의 생각에서 온다.

Our current stress comes from our thinking that there is not enough time.
 우리말을 영어로 옮기기

 그녀가 사임할 것이라는 소문이 있다.

There are rumors that she will resign.

 그 시스템이 변경되어야 한다는 제안은 거부되었다.

The proposal that the system should be changed was rejected.

 신이 사람을 만들었다는 생각은 구식이 되었다.

The idea that God created man became old-fashioned.

어느 길로 가야 하나요?

Language

As we know, Americans and British both speak in English. However, there are some important differences between British and American English, so they sometimes seem like totally different languages. First, the pronunciations are very different. Often, Americans tend to drop the consonant which comes right after certain consonants, which make sounds of /t/, /th/, /d/, etc. For example, when they say "I don't know", it sounds like "I dunno." On the contrary, the British usually articulate all the letters without dropping any sounds. Second, British and American English often use different words for the same things. For example, the vocabulary for cars and roads is very different. While Americans use 'highway' to name a certain type of road, the British call the same road 'motorway.' While Americans drive trucks, the British drive lorries. American people call the front of the car a hood, but the British call it a bonnet.

1   **Choose the best main idea of this passage.**

① the history of English   ② two main dialects of English
③ the sound system of English   ④ various sounds and meanings of English
⑤ the differences between American English and British English

2   American English와 British English의 구분이 잘못된 것은?

American		British
① highway	...	motorway
② I dunno	...	I don't know
③ hood	...	bonnet
④ truck	...	lorry
⑤ without dropping any sounds	...	to drop the consonant

Check Your
VOCABULARY!

seem like	totally	pronunciation	tend to
consonant	certain	on the contrary	articulate
vocabulary	name	lorry	bonnet

구문으로 익히는 **Writing & Speaking**

명사 바로 뒷자리에 있는 관계대명사 which

⬇ **명사 뒷자리**
Wind power is a source of energy which people can depend on in the future.
풍력은 미래에 사람들이 의존할 수 있는 에너지원이다.

⬇ **명사 뒷자리**
This is the taxi which hit the old man.
이것이 그 노인을 친 택시이다.

영어는 우리말(토씨어)과 달리 정해진 자리에서만 그 뜻을 나타낼 수 있다. which가 명사 바로 뒷자리에 떡하니 문장을 데리고 있는 경우 which 안의 동사를 우리말 '~하는, ~할, ~했던'으로 해석하여 앞에 있는 명사를 꾸며준다. 명사를 꾸며주는 역할을 한다고 해서 형용사절이란 말도 쓴다.

의존할 수 있다 + ~하는
➡ 의존할 수 있는

(S) can depend on + **which**
명사 + **which** (S) can depend on

우리말은 단어 자체를 형용사 어미로 바꿔 앞에서 뒤에 있는 명사를 꾸미며 '~하는, ~할, ~했던'으로 수식한다. 영어는 '의존할 수 있는'이란 말을 만들려면 반드시 which가 이끄는 문장이 명사 바로 뒷자리에 위치가 고정되어야 한다.

Practice

1 Parents set the stage upon which the friendships of their children are played out.

해석 ◐ _____

2 내 여자친구는 ₘy girlfriend 항상 나에게 값싼 which were cheap 선물을 presents 사주었다 bought.

영작 ◐ _____

Super Speaking

1단계 : 처음 우리말과 영문을 보면서 영어로 말해본다.
2단계 : 영문을 손으로 가리고 우리말만 보면서 완전한 영어로 말할 수 있도록 3~4회 반복한다.

 오직 64명만을 태우는 Sea Cloud호를 타고 여행하는 것은 특별한 경험이다.

A journey aboard the Sea Cloud which carries only 64 passengers is a special experience. 우리말을 영어로 옮기기

 10년간 네가 사용했던 그 녹음기는 수리할 수 없다.

The tape recorder which you used for 10 years can't be repaired.

 선생님은 스스로를 소진함으로써 다른 것들을 밝혀주는 양초와 같다.

The teacher is like the candle which lights others by consuming itself.

 친절은 귀 먼 사람들이 들을 수 있고 눈먼 사람들이 볼 수 있는 언어이다.

Kindness is the language which the deaf can hear and the blind can see.

Teen Life

I was an art student. Everybody told me I had a talent for painting. Tempted by fame, I told my art professor that I wanted to leave university to go to Paris, the home of many well-known artists. (a) Also, I was an acknowledged student by the professor of the university.

(b) "Jim," Professor Turner said, "I believe you've mastered the basic skills of painting, but there are many more things you need to learn about art and life. If you finish your studies at university, I will teach you all that you need."

I didn't listen to him, however, choosing the possibility of fame instead. Professor Turner said, "You are making a mistake, Jim, and perhaps some day _____."

(c) I went to Paris anyway. I was sure I'd become a famous artist quickly. Overconfident of my skills, I didn't work hard and too frequently went to the movies and to parties with my friends. One of them, who painted for art's sake alone, told me that I should work harder and quit painting for money. (d) Ignoring his advice, I wasted my time and continued to paint what I thought was popular. Gradually, however, people lost interest in my paintings. (e) I became penniless and finally stopped painting. Now I am working in an office but I still think about my art. All my life, I'll regret not taking <u>my teacher's advice</u> seriously. 기출

1 Jim에 관한 설명 중, 이 글의 내용과 일치하지 <u>않는</u> 것은?

① He was once expected to be a good painter.

② He went to Paris after getting his university degree.

③ He was overconfident in his ability to paint.

④ In Paris, he painted for money rather than for art's sake.

⑤ Now he is making a living as an office worker.

2 밑줄 친 <u>my teacher's advice</u>의 내용으로 가장 적절한 것은?

① 화가로서의 소양을 더 쌓아라.

② 귀국해서 후학 양성에 힘써라.

③ 자신의 개성을 최대한 살려라.

④ 대중 예술에 집착하지 말라.

⑤ 파리에서 화가로 성공하라.

3 (a)~(e) 중, 이 글의 전체 흐름과 관계 <u>없는</u> 문장은?

① (a)　　　　② (b)　　　　③ (c)

④ (d)　　　　⑤ (e)

4 **Choose the best answer to fill in the blank.**

① you may become a famous artist

② you'll be better than me

③ you'll miss your friends a lot

④ you'll be homesick

⑤ you'll regret your decision

Check Your
VOCABULARY!

talent

tempt

fame

professor

well-known

acknowledged

master

possibility

make a mistake

be sure

quickly

overconfident

frequently

for one's sake

quit

ignore

gradually

penniless

regret

seriously

degree

make a living

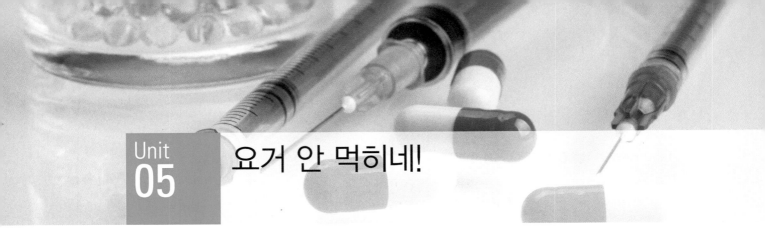

요거 안 먹히네!

After watching television all day, Kelly remembered (A) what / that she was going to have a test at school the next day. She also remembered that she had not finished her homework. It was already midnight, so Kelly was too sleepy to do her homework and study for the test. However, she did not want to screw up on the test and be punished for not doing the homework. She thought, "I (B) would / could rather not go to school tomorrow." However, she knew her parents would not allow her to miss school without a good reason. So she decided to pretend to be sick.

The following morning, Kelly's mother woke her up as usual. Kelly opened her eyes and said in a weak voice, "Mom, I don't feel well. I am afraid I can't go to school today. My stomach hurts." Then Kelly made a wry face as if she had stomach cramps.

"Oh dear, you must have a stomach virus! I'll get your father," said her mother with concern. When Kelly's father came in, he was not deceived by Kelly's expression at all. "Don't worry. I have some medicine for you," said her father. "It tastes so awful that you will lose your appetite for at least three days. But it is really (C) effecting / effective , so you don't have to miss school. But if you are still sick after taking the medicine, I will call the doctor and ask him to give you a couple of shots."

Hearing that, Kelly immediately jumped up from her bed and said, "Oh, never mind, I feel better already!"

1 이 글의 분위기로 가장 적절한 것은?

① indifferent

② humorous

③ serious

④ exhausted

⑤ logical

2 **What is the moral of this passage?**

① Tricking others is troublesome.

② Attend school in any situation.

③ Always be honest.

④ Be more intelligent.

⑤ Don't watch television.

3 (A), (B), (C)의 각 네모 안에서 어법에 맞는 표현을 골라 짝지어진 것으로 가장 적절한 것은?

	(A)		(B)		(C)
①	what	...	would	...	effective
②	what	...	could	...	effecting
③	that	...	could	...	effecting
④	that	...	would	...	effective
⑤	that	...	would	...	effecting

4 이 글의 내용과 일치하지 <u>않는</u> 것은?

① Kelly needed an acceptable reason to miss school.

② Kelly doesn't like injections.

③ Kelly's mom wasn't fooled by Kelly's expression.

④ Kelly's idea wasn't successful.

⑤ Kelly was scared of the test and punishment.

Check Your VOCABULARY!

screw up

be punished

would rather

allow

miss

pretend to

as usual

wry

as if

stomach cramp

concern

deceive

expression

awful

appetite

at least

effective

a couple of shots

immediately

never mind

indifferent

exhausted

logical

trick

injection

fool

WORD REVIEW

A Translate into English.

1 꼬리표 _____

2 광고하다, 선전하다 _____

3 세정제, 세제 _____

4 ～에서 회복하다 _____

5 우울한 _____

6 ～하는 경향이 있다 _____

7 부정적인 감정 _____

8 기꺼이 ～하다 _____

9 실내에서 _____

10 자음 _____

11 어휘, 단어 _____

12 재능 _____

13 잘 알려진 _____

14 인정받은 _____

15 후회하다 _____

16 평판, 명성 _____

17 망치다 _____

18 걱정 _____

19 몹시 나쁜 _____

20 식욕 _____

21 마음을 끌다, 유혹하다 _____

22 숙달하다 _____

23 점진적으로 _____

24 ～인 체하다 _____

25 마치 ～처럼 _____

B Translate into Korean.

1 awesome _____

2 content _____

3 stomachache _____

4 as a matter of fact _____

5 liquid _____

6 influence _____

7 in contrast _____

8 as usual _____

9 seem like _____

10 articulate _____

11 lighten _____

12 affect _____

13 pronunciation _____

14 overconfident _____

15 possibility _____

16 penniless _____

17 deceive _____

18 never mind _____

19 a couple of shots _____

20 stomach cramp _____

21 totally _____

22 on the contrary _____

23 frequently _____

24 for one's sake _____

25 expression _____

C Choose the correct answers to each question.

1 Stick the stamps on and then drop the letter into the _____ over there.

① mailbox   ② label

③ content   ④ awesome

2 The use of _____ to clean fruits and vegetables can also cause water pollution.

① determine   ② detergent

③ taboo   ④ appetite

3 One letter can have several _____.

① pronunciations   ② appetite

③ articulate   ④ vocabulary

D Translate into English or Korean.

1 The children were worried that there were no life guards on duty at the pool.

_____

2 They want to know what they will get from their parents before Christmas day.

_____

3 한국 연의 모양은 그 연들이 바람을 잘 이용하게 할 수 있도록 가능케 해 주는 과학적인 원리에 기초합니다.

(make good use of, enable, which)

The shape of Korean kites are based on scientific principles _____

_____ the wind.

E Choose the correct words to fill in the blanks.

1 One of the things _____ they talked about was how to enforce laws against dumping waste into water sources.

① so   ② which   ③ what   ④ how

2 • Nobody knows _____ will happen next.

• I know _____ you did last summer.

① so   ② that   ③ what   ④ which

3 When doing anything, just focus on _____ you are doing.

① so   ② that   ③ what   ④ which

4 다음 중 that이 생략되었을 곳을 고르시오.

Everyone knows (①) we need somebody to help (②) us to build (③) a tree house for (④) my younger brother.

F Match each word with its synonym and antonym (one synonym and one antonym for each word).

1 regret

2 advertise

3 difference

4 fame

5 immediately

a. distinctness

b. be satisfied with

c. at once

d. publicize

e. correspondence

f. later

g. feel sorry about

h. celebrity

i. hide

j. obscurity

★ 〈목적격 관계대명사〉 또는 〈주격 관계대명사 + be동사〉는 생략 가능하다.

We study philosophy because of the mental skills **(which / that)** it helps us develop.

우리는 우리를 발전하게 도와주는 정신적 기술 때문에 철학을 공부한다.

It is so easy to include hidden assumptions **(which / that)** you do not see but **(that are / which are)** obvious to others.

당신은 알지 못하지만 다른 사람들에게는 명백한 숨겨진 가정들을 포함하는 것은 매우 쉽다.

★ 가정법 과거완료(과거 사실의 반대) : 〈If + 주어 + had + p.p. ~, 주어 + 조동사 과거 + have + p.p. ~〉

If you **had turned** a light toward Mars that day, it **would have reached** Mars in 186 seconds.

만약 당신이 그 날 화성을 향해 빛을 쏘았다면, 그것은 186초 만에 화성에 도달하였을 것이다.

If Clauss **hadn't reacted** so quickly and decisively, there **would have been** two drownings instead of one.

만약 Clauss가 그렇게 빠르고 결정적으로 대처하지 않았다면 익사 사고가 하나가 아니라 둘이었을 것이었다.

★ 〈전치사 + 관계대명사〉의 형태의 관계대명사절에는 다른 관계대명사절과 달리 완전한 문장이 온다. that 앞에는 전치사가 올 수 없음을 주의하자.

The phrase "The Empire **on which** the sun never sets" was used to describe the Spanish Empire in the 16th century. (on that → X)

'해가 절대 지지 않는 제국'이라는 문구는 16세기 스페인 제국을 표현하기 위해 사용되었다.

1 다음 중 생략 가능한 것은?

This is not the dish which I ordered ten minutes ago.
　　①　　　②　　　③　　　　　　　　④

2 다음 괄호 안에서 알맞은 것을 고르시오.

If I had been able to reach the remote control, I never [would see / would have seen] this movie.

3 다음 괄호 안에서 알맞은 것을 고르시오.

This is the book in [that / which] I can find the clearest and most concise explanation.

Daily Assignment Book

Homeroom teacher : _____

공부습관의 최강자가 되라!

수업일	Contents (수업내용)		Homework (과제물)	Check (숙제검사)	
월 일				Done	Didn't do
월 일				Done	Didn't do
월 일				Done	Didn't do
나의 학습 아킬레스건	나의 취약 부분은?			Done	Didn't do
	해결 방법은?			Done	Didn't do
			Parent's Signature		

※ 학생들이 학원에서 공부한 내용입니다. 바쁘시더라도 관심을 갖고 확인해 주십시오.

Love from Valentine

서양에서는 2월 14일을 발렌타인데이라고 하여 아주 특별하게 보냅니다. 이날 사람들은 발렌타인데이 축하 카드를 연인, 친구들, 가족들에게 보내죠. 상점들은 2월 14일이 되기 훨씬 전부터 발렌타인 용품과 장식을 팔고 어린 학생들은 교실을 하트와 레이스로 장식을 합니다. 그리고 사람들은 각자의 친구들에게 사탕, 꽃, 특별한 선물을 주곤 합니다. 이렇게 서양에서 시작된 발렌타인데이 행사는 이제 우리나라에서도 시끌벅적하게 지나가는 날 중에 하나가 되었습니다. 발렌타인데이엔 초콜릿이 빠질 수 없죠. 이날이 되면 길거리마다 초콜 릿으로 꾸며져 있으며 사람들은 사랑하는 사람들을 위해서 그중 제일 예쁘고 맛있는 초콜릿을 구입합니다. 초콜릿처럼 달콤하고 풍만한 깊은 맛을 내는 특별하고 기분 좋은 하루를 보내기 위해서죠.

발렌타인데이의 기원에 관해 많은 이야기들이 있습니다. 어떤 전문가들은 로마의 성발렌타인(St. Valentine)에서 시작되었다고 합니다. 발렌타인은 당시 황제 클라디우스는 젊은 청년들을 군대로 끌어들이고자 결혼금지령을 내렸는데 이에 반대하고 서로 사랑하는 젊은이들을 결혼시켜준 죄로 A.D. 269년 2월 14일에 순교한 사제의 이름입니다. 그는 그 당시 간수의 딸에게 "Love from Valentine"이라는 편지를 남겼고, 발렌타인데이에 사랑의 메시지를 전하는 풍습의 기원이 되었죠. 발렌타인데이가 연인들의 날로 알려져 있는 것도 이런 까닭이라고 추측됩니다. 어떤 이들은 발렌타인의 죽음을 추모하는 의식을 2월 중순에 가진 것이 유래라고 하기도 하고, 어떤 이들은 이교도 축제인 Lupercalia를 기독교화하기 위해 발렌타인 축제를 행사화하였다고도 합니다. 당시 Lupercalia 축제에 도시의 젊은 여자들은 자기 이름을 큰 항아리에 적어 넣고 남자들이 항아리에서 이름표를 고르는 짝짓기 행사가 있었다고 합니다. 그 결과로 결혼까지 가는 경우가 많았다고 하네요. 이런 상황들을 교황이 보기에 이 축제가 매우 비기독교적이며 위법적이라고 생각하여 서기 498년에 2월 14일을 St. Valentine's Day로 선언하여 남녀간의 사랑을 표현하는 날로 삼았다고 전해집니다. 사실 영국과 프랑스에서 2월 14일을 이른바 새들의 짝짓기가 시작되는 날이라고 하며 그래서 이날을 그날로 정한 것이라고 하기도 합니다.

Chapter 03

Unit 01 배우고 익힌 자

Unit 02 광고

Unit 03 자신의 일을 즐겨라!

Unit 04 무위자연

Unit 05 물에 뛰어드는 용기

 단원 어휘

- poverty n. 빈곤, 가난
- dutiful a. 성실한, 충성된
- obedient a. 순종하는
- ruler n. 통치자, 지배자
- relatively adv. 상대적으로, 비교적
- inform v. 알리다, 정보를 제공하다
- cost-effective a. 비용 효율이 높은
- intend to ～할 의도하다
- satisfaction n. 만족
- devote v. 헌신하다, 바치다
- means n. 수단, 방법
- atmosphere n. 대기, 분위기, 환경
- release v. 방출하다 n. 석방, 해방
- consequently adv. 결과적으로
- emission n. 방사, 방출
- isolate v. 고립시키다, 분리시키다
- notify v. 통지하다, 알리다
- immediately adv. 즉시
- rescue v. 구조하다 n. 구조
- risk n. 위험, 모험 v. 위태롭게 하다
- courageous a. 용감한

Mini Quiz Draw a line from each word on the left to its definition on the right. Then, use the numbered words to fill in the blanks in the sentences below.

1	ruler	a. as a result
2	intend to	b. someone who governs a state or nation
3	satisfaction	c. without delay
4	consequently	d. to have something in your mind as a plan or purpose
5	immediately	e. able to face danger, difficulty, uncertainty, or pain
6	courageous	f. a feeling of pleasure that comes when a need or desire is fulfilled

7 She got great _____ from helping people to learn.

8 The telephone rang, and he answered it _____.

9 We do have very good normal relations with China, and we _____ keep on having those relations.

10 He was wrong, and _____ enough to admit it.

11 The _____ of the country was designated as king.

12 He did well on his test and _____ felt better.

무관한 문장 고르기

모든 글의 단락은 각각의 문장들이 유기적인 통일성을 가지고 하나의 주제를 뒷받침하게 된다. 무관한 문장 고르기는 보통 주제문 이후에 주제문을 보충 설명해주는 문장들을 나열하다가, 주제문에 등장하는 핵심어구는 등장하나 주제 내용의 흐름과는 관계없고 주제문의 주장을 뒷받침해주지 못하는 문장을 삽입해 놓고 이 문장을 골라내는 문제이다.

무관한 문장 고르기 유형의 급소

❶ **글의 주제를 파악한다.** 이러한 유형의 문제의 글은 90% 이상 두괄식이므로 첫 문장에서 핵심어나 주제를 찾고, 그 뒤에 어떤 내용들이 연결될지를 논리적으로 생각해야 한다. 만약 주제문이 없다면 첫 문장에서 핵심어를 찾아내어 그 핵심어에 벗어난 문장을 찾으면 된다.

❷ **지시어나 대명사, 연결사 등의 쓰임에 주의해야 한다.** 지시어나 대명사가 쓰였다면 지칭하는 바를 찾아내어, 글 전체와 일관성이 있는지를 확인한다. 한편, 영어의 모든 연결사는 문장과 문장 간의 논리적 연결고리 역할을 하므로, 연결사를 중심으로 앞뒤 문장의 논리적인 일관성이 있는지와 그것이 주제와 관련이 있는지를 따져 보아야 한다. 특히 however, but 등의 대조를 나타내는 연결사는 앞 내용과 상반된 내용을 이끈다 하더라고 그것이 주제와 관련되어 있는 진술이라면, 논리적 일관성에 어긋나는 것은 아니다.

❸ **주어나 시제의 일관성도 중요 단서가 될 수 있다.** 특정 주제에 대한 보충 설명이 일관되게 이어지다가 갑자기 앞 문장과 다른 주어가 등장한다거나 과거시제로 진행되다가 현재시제 등이 나온다면, 바로 그 부분이 논리적 일관성을 해치는 문장이 아닐까 하고 꼼꼼히 따져 보아야 한다.

❹ **글의 전개 방식을 이해한다.** 글은 몇 가지의 전개 방식에 따라 쓰이는데, 이러한 전개 방식을 알아두면 글의 요지를 빨리 파악할 수 있고, 주제에서 벗어나 있는 문장을 쉽게 찾을 수 있다.

❺ **반복되는 어휘나 표현에 주의한다.** 각각의 문장마다 반복되는 어휘나 표현이 있다. 이 어휘나 표현이 전체 글에서 말하고자 하는 내용을 전달하기 위해서 쓰인 것인지, 아니면 표현은 동일하지만 내용이 전혀 다른 것인지를 판단하도록 한다. 특히 요즘은 이렇게 동일한 표현이 가리키는 내용이 전체 글과 관련이 있는지의 여부를 묻는 것이 일반적인 경향이다.

다음 글에서 전체 흐름과 관계 없는 문장은? 기출문제

The rainforests are full of plants and animals that need each other and help each other. For example, the ant plant has tunnels in its stems which are just right for ants to live in. ① The ants put bits of dead insects inside some of the tunnels, and then the ant plant uses them for food. ② The ants also look after a caterpillar which lives inside the ant plant and eats its leaves. ③ Because of this, the ants come out of the ground and attack the caterpillar. ④ In return, the caterpillar makes a special honey mixture which the ants eat. ⑤ In this way, these three all live together in harmony.

*caterpillar 나비 · 나방의 유충, 애벌레

[논리독해]

Key-word : 첫 문장 (열대우림에서 서로 도우며 공생하는 동식물들)

수험생의 눈

▶ 글의 주제나 요지를 파악한다.

▶ 글 전체의 구성 방식을 파악한다.

▶ 부정어구나 논리적으로 모순되는 표현에 유의한다. 이 글은 동물과 식물의 공생 관계에 대한 것인데 개미가 유충을 '돌본다(look after)'라는 표현을 썼는데, ③에서는 '공격한다(attack)'라는 어휘를 사용한 것은 논리적인 모순을 불러일으킨다.

배우고 익힌 자

History &
Human

"Confucius" is a Latin form of the Chinese name "kung-fu-tse." Confucius was a great Chinese thinker, who was born in 557 B.C. In his time, China had a lot of problems. The government was weak, and there were crimes everywhere. People suffered from poverty. Confucius's father died when he was only three years old. He was dutiful and obedient to his mother. When Confucius grew up, he became a prudent, thoughtful and studious person. He liked to watch and study people and their behavior. Confucius thought that he could help others live better lives, so he left his family. He taught people to be honest and considerate. He thought the most important thing in one's life was to obey his or her parents and rulers. In addition, he believed a mature person never gets angry. Most of his lessons are very similar to that of Jesus Christ. One goes, "Don't make others do what you don't want to do." Later, a lot of people followed Confucius, and his ideas and beliefs became the school of Confucius, which is called "Confucianism." Confucius died in 479 B.C.

1　**What kind of writing is this paragraph?**

① report　　　　② autobiography　　③ biography
④ description　　⑤ poem

2　**What would be Confucius's article of faith?**

① to think cautiously before making a decision
② to study people and their behavior
③ to obey one's parents and rulers
④ to help poor people
⑤ to be a prudent, thoughtful and studious person

**Check Your
VOCABULARY!**

Confucius	thinker	suffer from	poverty
dutiful	obedient	prudent	studious
considerate	obey	mature	Confucianism

쉼표 뒷자리에서 부연 설명하는 관계사

쉼표 뒷자리 ⬇

Teachers must maintain a good relationship with the parents, who are also an important part of the total community.

교사들은 부모들과 좋은 관계를 유지해야 하는데, 이는 부모들 역시 모두 지역 공동체에서 중요한 역할을 하기 때문이다.

⬇ **쉼표 뒷자리**

The man, who looks scary, is in fact very shy.

그 남자, 그런데 그는 무섭게 보이는데, 사실은 매우 부끄러움을 탄다.

쉼표(,) 바로 뒷자리에 관계대명사나 관계부사가 있으면 보충 설명하는 계속적 용법이다. 선행사에 대한 부연 설명을 나타내므로 앞에서부터 차례대로 해석한다. '그런데 앞 단어(그 사람/그것)'로 해석한다. 앞의 명사를 다시 읽고 쭉 해석한다.

Practice

1 Vicky, who is wearing a heavy winter coat, is practicing on the stage for tomorrow's presentation of a play.

해석 ◐ _____

2 그 소녀는 귀신을 the ghost 좋아했다, 그런데 그 귀신은 그 애와 놀아줬다 played with her.

영작 ◐ _____

Super Speaking 1단계 : 처음 우리말과 영문을 보면서 영어로 말해본다.
2단계 : 영문을 손으로 가리고 우리말만 보면서 완전한 영어로 말할 수 있도록 3~4회 반복한다.

  이를 드러내면서 웃는 Susan의 미소는 큰데, 그녀의 이는 여전히 상태가 좋다.

Susan's smile is big, showing off all her teeth, which are still in good condition. 우리말을 영어로 옮기기

  마더 테레사, 그런데 그녀는 1979년에 노벨 평화상을 수상했는데, 카톨릭 수녀였다.

Mother Teresa, who won the Novel peace prize in 1979, was a Catholic nun.

  Tom은, 그런데 그는 불어와 이탈리아어를 말하는데, 관광 안내원으로 일한다.

Tom, who speaks French and Italian, works as a tourist guide.

  우리는 하얏트 호텔에서 머물렀는데, 그런데 그것은 우리가 온라인에서 매우 합리적인 가격으로 예약한 것이다.

We stayed at the Hyatt Hotel, which we booked online at a very reasonable rate.

Advertisement

Television advertisements are not as effective as video advertisements. In the first place, it is very expensive to advertise on television. In addition, even if a company spends a lot of money to advertise on television, they have no guarantee that enough customers will see the advertisements. The problem is that they cannot make people's eyes fixed on the ads, because television has many channels. Moreover, there are some people who do not have a television set. So, actually, advertisers have no idea if anyone actually sees the television ads. In addition, it is impossible to send the ads exclusively to the people who are likely to buy their products. Also, television ads are relatively shorter than video ads. It is hard to make people buy a product in less than a minute. In contrast, video advertisements can be as long as the advertiser wants them to be, but most of them are usually not longer than 7 minutes. As a result, customers can be more informed about the product when they see the advertisement on video rather than on television. In addition, using a video tape to advertise is much more cost-effective, because manufacturers can send the video advertisement to people who really intend to buy their product.

1   **What is the best title of this paragraph?**

① Ads: Present and Future   ② Television: Present and Future

③ Ads: Video or television?   ④ Video: Problem and Solution

⑤ Products: Buy or Sell?

2   **이 글의 내용과 일치하지 않는 것은?**

① It is expensive to advertise on television.

② It is possible to gather enough customers through ads on TV.

③ Advertisers cannot send their ads selectively if they advertise on TV.

④ One minute is not enough to get information about a product.

⑤ Video ads make it possible to contact the potential buyers.

Check Your
VOCABULARY!

advertisement	guarantee	fixed	advertiser
exclusively	be likely to	product	relatively
inform	cost-effective	manufacturer	intend to

사역동사의 특징

          ↓ make   X   Y

A symphony orchestra can make *a whole building* ring with music.
교향악단은 건물 전체를 음악으로 울리게 만들 수 있다.

        ↓ let   X   Y₁   Y₂

Don't let *your children* make too much noise or jump around in a restaurant.
당신의 아이들이 식당에서 너무 떠들거나 뛰어다니게 내버려 두지 마라.

대표적인 사역동사로는 make, have, let이 있으며 기본적으로 '누구에게 ~를 시키다'의 뜻이다. 대표적인 문장으로 목적어와 목적격 보어의 관계가 '능동'인 경우에는 목적격 보어 자리에 '동사원형'을 취한다. 둘의 관계가 '수동'인 경우에는 목적격 보어 자리에 'ed/en(과거분사 p.p.)'이 온다.

전체 건물이 울리다 만들다 + ~하게(시키다)
➡ 전체 건물이 울리게 만들다
a whole building ring + make
➡ **make** a whole building **ring**

사역동사 make/have/let 뒤에는 목적어가 온다. 이 목적어의 동작을 하게끔 하기 위해 목적어 바로 뒤 목적격 보어 자리에 동사원형을 쓴다. 우리말 '(목적어)가 ~(목적격 보어)하게 시키다/만들다'의 뜻이 된다. 목적어를 X로 하고 목적격 보어 동사원형을 Y로 하면 X와 Y가 연이어 나오는데, 'X에게 Y하라고 시키다'의 의미를 가진다.

Practice

1 Our teacher made us write it out five times again.

해석 ◯ _____

2 나는 Mark에게 나의 자전거를 ~my bicycle~ 고치도록 ~fix~ 시킬 것이다 ~will have~.

영작 ◯ _____

Super Speaking

1단계 : 처음 우리말과 영문을 보면서 영어로 말해본다.
2단계 : 영문을 손으로 가리고 우리말만 보면서 완전한 영어로 말할 수 있도록 3~4회 반복한다.

여전히 다른 뱃노래들은 선원들이 그들의 고된 일을 불평하도록 허락한다.

Still other Chanteys let sailors complain about their hard lives.

우리말을
영어로
옮기기

아빠가 내게 이 차를 쓰게끔 해주셨어.

My father let me use this car.

온라인 쇼핑은 우리가 가구, 음식, 심지어 애완동물까지도 살 수 있게 해준다.

Online shopping allows us to buy furniture, food, and even pets.

선생님은 그 학생이 진실을 말하도록 시켰다.

The teacher made the student tell the truth.

Unit 03 자신의 일을 즐겨라!

Lifestyle

There are so many reasons why people need to work. There are some people who work, not necessarily for money or any other material values, but for their own joy or self-satisfaction. A good example of those who could not live without working might be Wolfgang Amadeus Mozart, one of the greatest composers in history. He could care less about money as long as he could buy a piece of paper and some ink to write music. Another good example is Jack London. Jack London, an American writer, devoted his whole life to writing stories about ordinary people who tried their best to achieve their goals in life. In addition, Roald Amundsen, the great Norwegian explorer, spent his whole life exploring the world. He was the first person who reached both the North and the South Pole. The people mentioned here tried to get excitement through their work. They considered work as a means of amusement. It made their life enjoyable; it gave them reasons to live. In other words, _____ were the same for them.

1 **Choose the best phrase to fill in the blank.**

① work and play   ② life and work   ③ truth and life

④ work and honor   ⑤ joy and effort

2 **From this paragraph, what can we know about the three people?**

① They were the best in their fields.

② They all sought the truth of life.

③ They all worked for money.

④ They sacrificed their personal lives.

⑤ They worked for their own joy.

Check Your VOCABULARY!

necessarily	material value	self-satisfaction	composer
devote	ordinary	achieve	explore
mention	excitement	means	amusement

구문으로 익히는 **Writing & Speaking**

those who

Heaven helps those who help themselves.
하늘은 스스로 돕는 자를 돕는다.

Those who wish to travel in Asia must learn how to use chopsticks. If they do not, they may starve to death.
아시아를 여행하고 싶어 하는 사람들은 젓가락을 어떻게 사용하는지 배워야 한다. 만약 배우지 않으면 굶어 죽을지도 모른다.

those who는 항상 함께 다니기 때문에 문장에서의 자리가 중요하지 않다. 눈으로 보거나 들을 때마다 those who는 '~하는 사람들(복수 취급)', he who는 '~하는 사람(단수 취급)'으로 해석해 주기만 하면 된다.

those who ~ (= people who~)
: ~하는 사람들

he who ~ (= a man who~)
: ~하는 사람

Practice

1 Those who understand their own history and the history of the world, will have an easier time anticipating what will happen in the future.

해석 ○ _____

2 다른 사람들을 도와주지 않는 don't help others 사람들은 다른 이들의 by others 도움을 받지 못할 것이다 won't be helped.

영작 ○ _____

Super Speaking 　1단계 : 처음 우리말과 영문을 보면서 영어로 말해본다.
　　　　　　　　　　2단계 : 영문을 손으로 가리고 우리말만 보면서 완전한 영어로 말할 수 있도록 3~4회 반복한다.

 물이 풍부한 지역의 사람들은 물이 부족한 지역에 사는 사람들에게 물이 얼마나 귀한 것인지를 모른다.

 땀을 많이 흘리는 사람들은 혈액이 정상인보다 적다.
Those who perspire a lot have less blood than normal.

 뱀한테 물려본 사람은 잔디를 피해간다.
He who was bitten by a snake avoids tall grass.

 열경련은 더울 때 실외에서 힘을 많이 써야 하는 사람들에게 주로 영향을 미친다.
Heat cramps primarily affect those who exert themselves outdoors in hot weather.

In regions where water is abundant, people fail to realize what a real luxury it is to those who live where it is scarce.

 우리말을
영어로
옮기기

무위자연

Environment

(A)

Scientists say that the temperature of the Earth is increasing because of the increasing amount of carbon dioxide in the atmosphere. Carbon dioxide is released when something is burned. Rising temperatures cause polar icebergs to melt, and consequently raise sea levels and flood coastal areas. In other words, we should reduce carbon dioxide emissions. One solution for this problem is to develop alternative energy sources, such as solar power and wind energy, to replace fossil fuels, which produce a lot of carbon dioxide.

(B)

It is reported that 35.2 million acres of tropical forests, the size of New York state, are cut down every year. In Central America, rain forests are deforested for cattle ranching. Elsewhere, forests are used to provide people with furniture, housing materials, paper, etc. _____, expanding populations and growing needs for farmland are also blamed for forest loss. At this point, half of the world's tropical forests are gone, and if the deforestation continues at the current rate, most of the world's rain forests will disappear by the end of this century. Thus, it is time to do something about it.

1 **Choose the appropriate subjects for (A) and (B).**

(A)	(B)
① Rise of Sea Levels	... Use of Natural Resources
② Air Pollution	... Lack of Farmland
③ New Energy Development	... Change of Temperature
④ Global Warming	... Decrease of Rainforests
⑤ Increase of CO_2	... Cause of Environmental Destruction

2 **What are the style of the each topic?**

(A)		(B)
① informative	...	ceremonial
② persuasive	...	persuasive
③ informative	...	narrative
④ persuasive	...	ceremonial
⑤ ceremonial	...	informative

3 **What is a possible common title for (A) and (B)?**

① Let's Save the Earth!
② Stop Using Fossil Fuels!
③ Keep the Earth Clean!
④ Let's Live on a Clean Earth!
⑤ Develop the Earth Effectively!

4 **Choose the best answer to fill in the blank in (B).**

① On the contrary
② For example
③ Furthermore
④ To begin with
⑤ Nevertheless

Check Your
VOCABULARY!

temperature

carbon dioxide

atmosphere

release

iceberg

melt

consequently

in other words

reduce

emission

alternative energy

solar power

replace

fossil fuel

acre

tropical forest

cut down

deforest

cattle ranching

provide A with B

expanding

blame for

be gone

deforestation

current rate

Unit 05

물에 뛰어드는 용기

Adventure

William Darling, the keeper of the Longstone Lighthouse in the early 19th century in England, (a) had a daughter called Grace. Their family lived on Farne Island off the coast of Northumberland. Often the sea was violent, and the island was isolated. But Grace (b) loved playing with the baby sea animals and enjoying nature.

On September 7, 1838, the steamship Forfarshire, sailing from Hull to Dundee in England, met a terrifying storm near Farne Island. Nine people on the ship cried for help and, finally, Grace heard them. She notified her father immediately. However, (c) there was no other person to help him, so he could not set out to rescue these people. Therefore, even though Mrs. Darling was against the idea, Grace decided to go with her father risking her life. Eventually, Grace and William rescued five passengers. Grace was worn out from the first trip, (d) so she could not make the second trip to rescue others. Therefore, (e) William and two men who rescued from the first trip went out again to bring back the remaining people to safety. Along with her father, Grace became famous and received the Gold Medal of the Royal Humane Society for her courageous and humane act. Alas, Grace died of tuberculosis four years later. But Grace and her courage have not been forgotten.

1 Grace Darling에 관한 이 글의 내용과 일치하지 <u>않는</u> 것은?

① Grace enjoyed her environment.

② She received the Gold Medal of the Royal Humane Society.

③ She was afraid of the violent sea.

④ Grace and her father rescued five people.

⑤ Grace's father was the keeper of the lighthouse.

2 **Choose the best description of 'Grace.'**

① She is a charming daughter who only knows her family.

② She is an energetic girl who raises baby sea animals.

③ She is a courageous girl who knows the importance of life.

④ She is an insatiable girl trying to receive the Gold Medal.

⑤ She is an ordinary girl living by the sea.

3 (a)~(e) 중 어법상 <u>어색한</u> 것을 찾아 바르게 고치시오.

➡ _____

4 **Choose the best title for this passage.**

① The Brutal Nature of England

② The Accommodation of Humans

③ Methods of Receiving a Gold Medal

④ The English Heroine of the Sea

⑤ Life of a Girl Called 'Grace'

WORD REVIEW

A Translate into English.

1 사상가, 사색가 _____

2 통치자, 지배자 _____

3 유교 _____

4 빈곤, 가난 _____

5 광고 _____

6 제조업자 _____

7 ～할 의도이다 _____

8 오로지, 독점적으로 _____

9 복종하다, 응하다 _____

10 부득이, 할 수 없이 _____

11 작곡가 _____

12 만족(감) _____

13 온도, 기온 _____

14 벌채하다 _____

15 현재 비율 _____

16 대체 에너지 _____

17 관리자 _____

18 고립시키다 _____

19 인도적 행위 _____

20 시작하다, 착수하다 _____

21 비교적, 상대적으로 _____

22 수단, 방법 _____

23 이산화탄소 _____

24 대체하다, 교체하다 _____

25 용기 있는 _____

B Translate into Korean.

1 dutiful _____

2 prudent _____

3 considerate _____

4 devote _____

5 product _____

6 cost-effective _____

7 be likely to _____

8 inform _____

9 explore _____

10 mention _____

11 release _____

12 consequently _____

13 iceberg _____

14 fossil fuel _____

15 cut down _____

16 rescue _____

17 lighthouse _____

18 terrify _____

19 worn out _____

20 along with _____

21 guarantee _____

22 emission _____

23 blame for _____

24 expanding _____

25 against _____

C Choose the correct answers to each question.

1 Confucius thought the most important thing in one's life was to _____ one's parents and rulers.

① suffer   ② release

③ isolate   ④ obey

2 One solution for carbon dioxide emissions is to develop _____ energy sources, such as solar power and wind energy, to replace fossil fuels.

① iceberg   ② fossil

③ deforestation   ④ alternative

3 The _____ team reported that they were approaching the site of the accident.

① receive   ② risk

③ notify   ④ rescue

D Translate into English or Korean.

1 These toys are from my relatives, who live with me.

_____

2 This is a new way to let people donate to charity while shopping online.

_____

3 결코 성공하지 못하는 사람들은 너무 빨리 그만두는 사람들이다. (those, never, make it)

_____ are the ones who quit too soon.

E Choose the correct words to fill in the blanks.

1 Hope, _____ seems like the thinnest little thread, is an incredibly powerful force leading us from the most horrible problems into a bright new day.

① who   ② whose ③ that   ④ which

2 In a survey published earlier this year, seven out of ten parents said they would never let their children _____ with toy guns.

① to play   ② playing

③ played   ④ play

3 Among _____ go to sea there are the explorers who discover new worlds, adding continents to the Earth and stars to the heavens.

① those   ② who those

③ those who   ④ me

F Match each word with its synonym and antonym (one synonym and one antonym for each word).

1 mature   a. extraordinary

               b. full-grown

               c. conform to

2 obey   d. normal

               e. childish

3 ordinary   f. reception

               g. disobey

4 emission   h. diffusion

               i. cut off

5 isolate   j. integrate

★ 〈be used to + -ing〉 vs 〈be used to + 동사원형〉 vs 〈used to + 동사원형〉

I **am used to** driving on the left because I've lived in Japan for 3 years.

나는 일본에서 3년간 살았기 때문에 도로 왼편으로 운전하는 것이 익숙하다.

This book should **be used to develop** your English skills.

이 책은 너의 영어 실력을 발달시키는 데 사용되어야 한다.

They **used to skip** their English classes so they failed the test.

그들은 영어수업을 빼먹곤 해서 시험에 낙제했다.

★ 명사절 if vs 조건절 if

I am not sure **if** this question will be on the test. 〈명사절〉

나는 이 문제가 시험에 나올지 안 나올지 확신이 없다.

If this question is on the test, I will not be able to solve it. 〈조건절〉

만약 이 문제가 시험에 나온다면 나는 풀지 못할 것이다.

★ 〈원급 비교문: as + 원급 + as〉 vs 〈비교급: 비교급 ~ than〉 vs 〈최상급: the + 최상급 + of/in + 명사구〉

Be **as specific as** possible. 가능한 구체적으로 되어야 한다.

If the movie calls for rivers, mountains, or jungles, it may be **cheaper** to film in real places **than** to build imitation scenery.

만약 영화에 강, 산 혹은 정글이 필요하면 실제 장소에 가서 촬영하는 것이 가짜 풍경을 만들어 내는 것보다 더 싸다.

1　다음 괄호 안에서 알맞은 것을 고르시오.

I'm used to [speak / speaking] English after I came to Canada.

2　다음 괄호 안에서 알맞은 것을 고르시오.

The contract will not be signed if your boss [won't / doesn't] show up in ten minutes.

3　다음 문장에서 틀린 부분을 찾아 바르게 고치시오.

Time is the most precious than all things.　➡ _____

Daily Assignment Book

Homeroom teacher : _____

공부습관의 최강자가 되라!

수업일		Contents (수업내용)	Homework (과제물)	Check (숙제검사)	
월	일			Done	Didn't do
월	일			Done	Didn't do
월	일			Done	Didn't do
나의 학습 아킬레스건	나의 취약 부분은?			Done	Didn't do
	해결 방법은?			Done	Didn't do
			Parent's Signature		

※ 학생들이 학원에서 공부한 내용입니다. 바쁘시더라도 관심을 갖고 확인해 주십시오.

혈액형이 성격에 미치는 영향을 믿으세요?

대부분 사람들은 혈액형 점이나 혈액형으로 사람의 성격을 믿습니다. 하지만 이러한 얘기들은 근거가 있는 사실들일까요? 유독 우리나라와 일본에만 있는 특이한 경우인데 외국에선 이런 현상을 이상하게 생각하고 있습니다. 단도직입적으로 말해서 혈액형과 성격과는 아무런 관계가 없습니다. 사람의 성격을 좌우하는 것은 혈액형이 아니라 그 사람이 살았던 환경적 여건에 영향을 많이 받는다고 합니다. 사람의 혈액형이 A형, B형, O형, AB형이다 해서 그 사람의 성격이 정해져 있진 않죠. 혈액형으로 다룬 점이나 또는 성격분류 같은 것에 얽매이지 않아도 됩니다. 그럼 혈액형 점이 형성된 기원을 알아보죠. 혈액형 점은 1971년 일본의 삼류작가인 노오미라는 사람이 단지 자기 생각대로 쓴 아무 근거 없는 하나의 이야기일 뿐입니다. 1971년 일본에 출판되기 시작하여 1980년 당시 일본에선 뜨거운 반응을 얻었고 그게 우리나라로 넘어와 많은 사람들에게 전달이 된 것이죠. 요즘에도 서점에서 찾아볼 수 있는 이 책은 마치 노오미가 대단한 과학자인 양 소개가 되어 있습니다.

노오미가 죽은 후에도 그의 자식이 이어서 그 이론을 부풀려나가서 오늘날까지 그 책이 존재한다고 추측됩니다. 그 책은 우리나라에 들어오면서는 마치 전 세계 과학자들이 열심히 연구한 결과 얻어진 무슨 과학이론이나 엄밀한 통계이론인 것처럼 포장되어 퍼지고 열렬한 신자들도 생겼습니다.

하지만 혈액형 점의 처음 시작과 어떻게 발견되었는지를 발견한 사람은 없죠. 혈액형 점의 실체가 없기 때문입니다. 엄밀한 통계학 조사로도 의학 조사로도 증명할 수 있는 단서는 아직 하나도 얻지 못했습니다. 즉 과학적 증명이 수십 년에 걸쳐 시도되어 왔지만 확실한 정답은 아직 찾지 못했죠. 그러므로, 혈액형 점이나 혈액형으로 성격을 나타내는 자료는 아직은 근거 없는 자료인 것입니다.

Chapter 04

Unit 01 불교가 힌두교에 밀려?

Unit 02 가장 한국적인 것

Unit 03 할로윈

Unit 04 신에 대한 도전

Unit 05 911 테러의 고통과 슬픔

단원 어휘

☐ meditation n. 명상, 묵상

☐ mistreat v. 학대하다

☐ prevalence n. 유행, 보급, 널리 퍼짐

☐ guarantee v. 보증하다 n. 보증

☐ vital a. 중요한

☐ categorize v. 분류하다, 범주에 넣다

☐ analysis n. 분석, 해석, 분해

☐ be composed of ~로 구성되다

☐ shorten v. 줄이다

☐ deceased n. 고인, 죽은 사람

☐ evil spirit 악령

☐ ethical a. 윤리적인

☐ morality n. 도덕, 윤리, 교훈

☐ ongoing a. 진행 중인

☐ oppose v. 반대하다

☐ penalize v. 유죄를 선고하다

☐ subdue v. 정복하다, 억제하다

☐ overthrow v. 뒤엎다, 전복하다

☐ collapse v. 붕괴하다, 무너지다

☐ broadcast v. ~을 방송하다

☐ subsequently adv. 그 후에

☐ mighty a. 강력한

Mini Quiz Draw a line from each word on the left to its definition on the right. Then, use the numbered words to fill in the blanks in the sentences below.

1	meditation	a. to send out radio or television programs
2	vital	b. continuing, or continuing to develop
3	categorize	c. very strong and powerful, or very big and impressive
4	ongoing	d. extremely important and necessary for something to succeed or exist
5	broadcast	
6	mighty	e. the practice of emptying your mind of thoughts and feelings, in order to relax completely
		f. to divide things or people into sets which they belong to.

7 The discussions are still _____.

8 The authority of the once _____ king rotted away.

9 Yoga involves breathing exercises, stretching, and _____.

10 Regular exercise is _____ for your health.

11 The interview was _____ live across Europe.

12 Participants are _____ into two groups according to gender.

독해에 진짜 필요한 **Reading Skill**

빈칸 추론

빈칸 완성 문제는 글 전체의 일관성을 정확하게 파악할 수 있는 추론 능력을 측정할 뿐만 아니라 어휘력, 문장 구성 능력 등을 측정할 수 있어 매년 가장 많이 출제되는 유형이다. 특히, 빈칸이 설정되는 문장은 주로 주제문이거나 적어도 주제와 밀접한 관련이 있는 문장으로, 핵심어(key-word)를 중심으로 주제나 요지를 파악해 내는 일이 가장 중요하다.

빈칸 추론 유형의 급소

❶ **빈칸이 설정된 문장이 주제문인 경우** – 대부분의 주제문은 글의 앞부분이나 뒷부분에 있지만 글의 내용을 요약하는 문장인 경우 주로 뒷부분에 위치한다.

❷ **핵심어(key-word)를 찾아라.** – 첫 문장에 주제와 밀접한 관련이 있는 핵심어가 있다. 빈칸이 마지막 문장에 있는 문제는 마지막에 핵심어가 있을 수도 있다. 지문의 마지막에 설정된 빈칸은 반드시 그 빈칸이 포함된 문장을 먼저 읽어야 한다. 그러면, 핵심어와 주제를 미리 예상할 수 있어 문제해결이 수월해진다. 결국 마지막 문장에 빈칸이 있는 단어 넣기 문제는 전체 글의 핵심어가 무엇인지를 찾으라는 것과 같다.

❸ **빈칸을 완성할 단서, 즉 지문의 주제나 요지를 찾아라.** – 단락 내의 모든 문장은 하나의 주제를 뒷받침해주는 문장들이므로 주제와 관련된 핵심어, 대명사, 유사한 문장구조 등이 반복해서 나오므로 내용 파악이 가능한 부분을 하나로 묶어 주제나 요지를 파악한다. 특히 빈칸이 글의 중반부에 있는 경우에는 빈칸에 들어갈 문장이 예시나 부연 설명일 가능성이 높다. 글의 주제를 파악한 후, 이를 각각의 예나 설명에 적용하는 방식으로 접근한다.

❹ **일화문은 마지막에 단서가 있다.** – 경험담 등에 근거한 일화문은 지문의 마지막 문장에 반드시 작가가 맺음말을 제시하므로 첫 문장에 설정된 빈칸을 채울 단서는 마지막 문장에서 얻을 수 있으며, 반대로 지문의 마지막에 있는 빈칸은 앞의 내용을 포괄할 수 있는 요지를 묻는 문제이다.

다음 글의 빈칸에 가장 적절한 것은? 기출문제

¹ Many difficulties and much stress today come from our thinking that there is not enough time. ² Time itself remains unchanged in the sense that it carries on in the same way as it has for millions of years. ³ We need to see that it is circumstances that are different and that our increased workloads put too much pressure upon us. ⁴ However, most of us try to adjust our attitudes and behaviors to a rapid pace of living and working. ⁵ The secret lies not in finding smart ways to do more, but in how we manage the relationship between the things we have to do and _____.

① the ability to do them

② the strong desire we have

③ the time available to do them in

④ the way to avoid stress

⑤ the place we live in

[논리독해]

Key-word : not enough time

1 어려움과 스트레스가 시간이 부족하다는 생각 때문이라는 통념(화제) 제시

2 시간은 변함없이 흐른다는 비판 제시

3 시간 때문이 아니라 환경과 과도한 작업량 때문이라는 비판 제시의 부연 설명

4 생활과 일의 속도에 적응하려 한다는 비판 반복 제시

5 주제문 (주제는 비판 부분에서 찾아야 한다.)

전재 방식

통념-비판, 문제-해결

Unit 01

불교가 힌두교에 밀려?

Religion

Buddhists believe that they can find inner peace within themselves. And they think that meditation and karma will lead them to Nirvana. Karma can be defined as the rewards or punishments for past actions. Karma simply explains that what exists now has resulted from what was before. A happy person who <u>treats</u> others with kindness and respect will meet people who respect him. This is called good karma. A person who mistreats others will be mistreated. This is called bad karma. Buddha did not wish his beliefs to replace other faiths. However, today there are over three hundred million Buddhists all around the world.

Even though Buddha was born an Indian prince, Buddhism lost its influence in India by the 8th century, partly because of the prevalence of Hinduism, and partly because of the rise of Islam. Nevertheless, his ideas and beliefs are worshiped mostly in China, Korea, Japan, and Southeast Asia. Buddhism is one of the major religious and moral forces in the world.

1 다음 중, 이 글의 밑줄 친 <u>treats</u>와 같은 의미로 쓰인 것은?

　① It is my family's turn to <u>treat</u> this time.

　② The patient was <u>treated</u> with new drugs.

　③ My mom <u>treated</u> me to a hamburger.

　④ He was upset by the way he was <u>treated</u>.

　⑤ I gave some <u>treats</u> to my dog for behaving so well.

2 **Write True or False.**

　(1) _____ By the 8th century, Buddhism lost its influence in India.

　(2) _____ Buddhists believe that mistreating others and karma will lead them to Nirvana.

　(3) _____ Today, there are over three million Buddhists all around the world.

Check Your VOCABULARY!

Buddhist	meditation	karma	Nirvana
define	mistreat	Buddha	prevalence
worship	religious	moral	force

양보의 부사절 even though, even if

He is a great athlete. Even though he has cancer, he did well in the soccer game.
그는 훌륭한 운동선수이다. 그는 암에 걸렸는데도 불구하고, 그는 축구경기에서 능숙하게 했다.

Even if the sun were to rise in the west, I would not change my mind.
비록 태양이 서쪽에서 뜬다 할지라도, 나는 내 마음을 바꾸지 않을 것이다.

부사절 접속사 even though는 문장 맨 앞에 위치하는 것이 보통이며, even though의 절 내용은 '사실'의 내용을 전달하고, 해석상 의미가 비슷해 보이지만 even if는 '가정'의 표현을 담고 있다.

| Practice

1 Childhood is an age of adventure. This is still true today, even though today the opportunities of adventure are considerably 상당히 fewer than they used to be 예전보다.

해석 ◉ _____

2 비록 귀신이 the ghost 방안으로 들어왔는데도 came into the room 불구하고 우리는 비명을 지르지 않았다 not scream.

영작 ◉ _____

| Super Speaking
1단계 : 처음 우리말과 영문을 보면서 영어로 말해본다.
2단계 : 영문을 손으로 가리고 우리말만 보면서 완전한 영어로 말할 수 있도록 3~4회 반복한다.

 때려 죽여도 나는 너한테 우리 누나 못준다.

 Even if you beat me to death, I wouldn't give my older sister to you.

우리말을
영 어 로
옮 기 기

 그들이 가난한데도 불구하고, 그들은 함께 있어 행복해 보인다.

Even though they are so poor, they seem happy together.

 그녀의 삶은 짧았지만 그녀는 세계 역사를 영원히 바꾸어 놓았다.

Even though her life was short, she changed the world history forever.

 가게 주인은 그가 전과자임에도 불구하고 그를 고용했다.

The shop keeper hired him even though he had a record.

가장 한국적인 것

The introduction of unique products alone does not guarantee market success. Another vital factor is increasing one's responsiveness to the markets by providing products suited for the local communities that make up the market. This means understanding that each country, community and individual has unique characteristics and needs; it requires _____.
In other words, one of the challenges is to avoid a one-size fits-all strategy that places too much emphasis on the "global" aspect alone. Even categorizing countries as "developed" or "emerging" is dangerous. Upon closer analysis, "emerging" countries are not only vastly different from one another, they are also composed of numerous unique individuals and communities. 기출

1   **Choose the best answer to fill in the blank.**
   ① global markets that expand rapidly
   ② employment of a one-size-fits-all strategy
   ③ sensitivity to regional and individual differences
   ④ resources that make the challenges meaningful
   ⑤ individual competition to raise productivity

2   **Choose the best main idea of the paragraph.**
   ① Local communities make up most of the global market.
   ② People should learn more about the customs of other countries.
   ③ The one-size-fits-all strategy has given a great success to the global marketing.
   ④ The idea of marketing should always be adaptable depending on individuals and communities.
   ⑤ Global marketing is a hard task for an ordinary company to begin.

Check Your
VOCABULARY!

introduction	guarantee	vital	responsiveness
make up	characteristic	require	one-size-fits-all strategy
emphasis	aspect	categorize	emerging
analysis	vastly	be composed of	numerous

명사 바로 뒷자리에서 명사를 설명하는 관계사 that

명사 뒷자리 ⬇

Most parents punish their children in the same way that they were punished by their parents.

대부분의 부모들은 그들이 자신의 부모들에 의해 벌을 받았던 것과 같은 방식으로 자녀들을 벌준다.

명사 뒷자리 ⬇

Although this may sound like an obvious first step, it is a step that many people ignore.

비록 이것이 명백한 첫 단계처럼 들릴지라도, 그것은 많은 사람들이 무시하는 단계이다.

관계대명사 that은 명사 바로 뒷자리에서 명사(선행사)를 꾸미는 형용사절 역할을 한다. 이러한 자리에 that은 해석상 의미가 없고 단지 기능상 꾸며주는 역할을 하는 장치에 불과하다.

무시하다 단계 + ~하는 ➡ 무시하는 단계
ignore + that ➡ 명사 + that (S) ignore

우리말은 명사를 설명할 때 모든 말이 명사 앞에서 마지막 꾸미는 말만 단어 자체를 형용사 어미인 '–ㄴ(니은)'으로 바꿔 꾸민다. 영어는 그 어떤 말도 명사 바로 뒷자리에 오면 마지막으로 꾸며주는 관계사절 안의 동사가 우리말 '–ㄴ(니은), ~하는, ~했던, ~았던'의 뜻으로 변한다. that이든, which든, where든 아무 뜻이 없고 자리를 알리는 역할만 한다.

Practice

1 Talking with people that have different backgrounds from your own can help broaden your conversational repertoire and your thinking.

해석 ◐ _____

2 황금알을 the golden eggs 낳는 lays 거위는 the goose 죽이지 마라 don't kill.

영작 ◐ _____

Super Speaking

1단계 : 처음 우리말과 영문을 보면서 영어로 말해본다.
2단계 : 영문을 손으로 가리고 우리말만 보면서 완전한 영어로 말할 수 있도록 3~4회 반복한다.

 직업을 고르는 데 있어서, 당신이 고려해야 할 첫 번째 것은 당신이 그 직업에 맞는지 맞지 않는지이다.

 나는 교통 혼잡이 없는 마을에서 거주하고 싶다.

I would like to dwell in a town where there is no traffic congestion.

 산악 지역들에서, 떨어지는 바로 그 눈 중 많은 부분은 얼음으로 굳어진다.

In mountainous regions, much of the snow that falls is compacted into ice.

 그 지연은 엉뚱한 물건을 배달한 납품업자 때문에 생긴 것이다.

The delay was caused by the supplier that delivered the wrong materials.

In choosing your occupation, the first thing that you have to consider is whether you are fit for it or not.

 우리말을 영어로 옮기기

Unit 03 할로윈

Origin

The name Halloween is shortened from "All-hallow-eve," since it is the day before All Hallow's Day. This is a festival held on October 31st to celebrate the end of the harvest season. Halloween has its origin in ancient Celtic culture. The Celts believed that the gap between the world of the living and that of the dead disappeared on October 31, and the dead would come back to life. They also believed that the deceased would bring them sickness. Therefore, they held a huge festival at night in order to placate the ghosts and evil spirits which might look for living victims. They also wore masks so that the evil spirits could not find them. The Romans also had a holiday in late October to celebrate their goddess Pomona, the goddess of fruits. Since the symbol of Pomona was an apple, candy apples became a common Halloween treat. Halloween seems to _____.
In Western culture, people tell spooky tales and scare each other on Halloween night. Halloween has become a holiday devoted to witches and ghosts.

1   **Which of the following is NOT true about Halloween?**
   ① Halloween is a combination of the Roman and Celtic festivals.
   ② People placated the ghosts and evil spirits for their harvest.
   ③ The origin of the Halloween is from ancient Celtic culture.
   ④ Celts thought that there was a gap between the world of the living and the dead.
   ⑤ People wore masks so that the evil spirits could not recognize them.

2   **Choose the best answer to fill in the blank.**
   ① be proceeded by the tradition of Celtic
   ② terrify people on the day because something harmful always happened
   ③ be a combination of the Roman and Celtic festivals
   ④ be opening a gap between death and living theoretically
   ⑤ be affected a lot by the Roman customs

Check Your VOCABULARY!

shorten	celebrate	harvest	origin
Celtic	deceased	placate	evil spirit
victim	treat	spooky	combination

구문으로 익히는 **Writing & Speaking**

... so that ~ 조동사

I got up early so that I might catch the first train.
나는 첫 기차를 타기 위해 일찍 일어났다.

I make it a rule to read the newspaper every morning in order not to
fall behind the times.
나는 시대에 뒤떨어지지 않기 위해 매일 아침 신문을 읽는 것을 규칙으로 하고 있다.

'so that ~ 조동사'는 'in order to = so as to = 이동 동사 + to부정사'와 비슷한 역할을
한다. 문장 중간에 so that이 나와서 조동사 may, can, will 등과 함께 쓰이면 '~하기
위하여'로 해석한다.

Practice

1   Language exists in order that people may communicate with each other. Often, however, language can be a source of misunderstanding, both between individuals and between peoples.

해석 ◐ _____

2   그 도둑은 사람들이 그를 알아보지 못하게 하려고 would not recognize him 검은 옷을 입었다 wore black.

영작 ◐ _____

Super Speaking
1단계 : 처음 우리말과 영문을 보면서 영어로 말해본다.
2단계 : 영문을 손으로 가리고 우리말만 보면서 완전한 영어로 말할 수 있도록 3~4회 반복한다.

   그 선생님은 그가 말한 것을 아이들이 이해할 수 있도록 천천히 말했다.

The teacher spoke slowly so that the children could understand what he said. 우리말을 영어로 옮기기

   리더스 다이제스트는 분량이 많은 책들을 요약해서 사람들이 빨리 읽을 수 있게 한다.
Reader's Digest abridges long books so that people can read them quickly.

   Nancy는 건강을 유지하기 위해 매일 수영을 한다.
Nancy swims every day so that she can stay healthy.

   그 범인은 경찰이 자신을 못 찾게 하기 위해 증거를 감췄다.
The criminal hid his tracks so that the police couldn't find him.

신에 대한 도전

Science

Some scientists are eager to produce a cloned living thing. However, this time they are not thinking of a sheep, but a human being. They do not bother about either medical risks or ethical issues. (a) People have been debating the morality of biological science and cloning. Some people believe that there is nothing unethical about cloning since it is nothing but practicing the human reproductive right. (b) The scientists who have conducted animal cloning research admit that there has been a high level of failure in their experiments. (c) A large number of animal fetuses died before birth and many others were born with abnormalities.

Yet, Boisselier, the director of the human cloning company Clonaid, said that human cloning experiments were already conducted. When asked for details, she just smiled and said: "I am doing it and hope I can publish the result soon and share it with you."

Panayiotis Michael Zavos, the director of the Andrology Institute in Lexington, and Dr. Severino Antinori of the University of Rome said they expected their ongoing human cloning research would benefit infertile men who want to have children. (d) However, they said they had not attempted to clone a human yet.

Most other scientists, religious groups and the government have opposed cloning. (e) A bill has passed in the U.S. House of Representatives to outlaw human cloning. Offenders will be penalized heavily.

1 **Which of the following is NOT in the passage?**

① There are debates about human-cloning.

② The questions about human cloning were answered easily.

③ Human cloning is now illegal.

④ Cloning of a human being has not been attempted yet.

⑤ Most scientists and religious groups, as well as the government, are against human cloning.

2 밑줄 친 a high level of failure가 의미하는 것으로 올바른 것은?

① There is a tribulation whenever failure occurs.

② The level of the experiment is very difficult.

③ Cloning experiments are likely to fail because scientists' research is different.

④ Cloning can fail easily because the animals' physical strength isn't very good.

⑤ Cloning has been successful in several mammals, including sheep, mice and cattle, but there is increasing evidence that it does not work for all species.

3 글의 흐름으로 보아, 다음 주어진 문장이 들어가기에 가장 적절한 곳은?

> On the contrary, others think it is an unethical and dangerous form of human experimentation.

① (a)   ② (b)   ③ (c)

④ (d)   ⑤ (e)

4 **Choose the best title of this passage.**

① Cloning of Animals

② Scientific and Medical Aspects of Human Cloning

③ Consequence of Human Cloning

④ A Long Way to Go: Human Cloning

⑤ Ban of Cloning in America

Check Your VOCABULARY!

be eager to

ethical

morality

biological

cloning

nothing but

human reproductive right

conduct

experimentation

fetus

abnormality

publish

andrology

ongoing

infertile

attempt to

oppose

bill

House of Representatives

outlaw

offender

penalize

tribulation

species

consequence

ban

Unit 05

911 테러의 고통과 슬픔

Terror

The world feels sorry! There is a war in Afghanistan. People in Afghanistan feel not just sorry. In fact, (A) they are sad and frightened. In 1997, the Taliban subdued most of Afghanistan. (a) The Taliban are the hardcore Muslims of Afghanistan. In that year, they were able to overthrow the government. (b) Since then, the (B) Taliban has ruled Afghanistan. Now, the Taliban seem to have gotten themselves in trouble. In 2001, there was a terrorist attack in the U.S.A. A good number of terrorists plotted to hijack a few American planes, and to crash the planes into crowded areas. As a result, the two World Trade Center buildings in New York collapsed. Also, the Pentagon in Washington D.C. was damaged. Due to this attack, a lot of people were injured and killed. (c) Later, Americans learned that _____ .

Now, it is time for the opposition to control Afghanistan. The Opposition Alliance in the north part of Afghanistan (C) decided to attacking the Taliban. (d) "Today we have a chance to defeat the Taliban and the terrorists," said Mohammed Fahim. He further added, "and we will pay whatever the cost." He has been the main leader of the opposition after the death of Ahmed Shah Masood. (D) His statement was broadcasted on national TV. (e) Subsequently, he was well known by people all over the world for his bravery. But the Opposition Alliance is not (E) the only enemy the Taliban will fight against. There are bigger and mightier enemies outside Afghanistan. The U.S. and some western European countries are trying to form a new government in Afghanistan. Mohammad Zahir Shah is a possible candidate for the next president of Afghanistan. Now, he is living in Rome.

1 (a)~(e) 중, 글의 전체 흐름과 관계 <u>없는</u> 문장은?

① (a)　　　　② (b)　　　　③ (c)

④ (d)　　　　⑤ (e)

2 **Choose the best title of this passage.**

① Ignorance of the Taliban

② Sorrow of the Dead People

③ A Plan to Revenge the Terrorists

④ The Opposition is about to Attack the Taliban

⑤ Remembrance of the Terrorist Attack in 2001

3 **Which is the most appropriate expression to fill in the blank?**

① the Pentagon building had poor construction

② they should obey the Taliban

③ they should organize a plan to hide underground

④ the Taliban were part of this terrorist plot

⑤ Taliban would make another attack

4 **Choose the grammatically wrong answer from the underlined choices in (A)~(E). And then correct the error.**

Check Your
VOCABULARY!

frightened

subdue

hardcore

Muslim

overthrow

rule

terrorist

a good number of

plot

hijack

collapse

due to

opposition

Opposition Alliance

defeat

statement

broadcast

subsequently

be known by

bravery

mighty

candidate

ignorance

sorrow

revenge

WORD REVIEW

A Translate into English.

1 불교도 _____
2 혹사하다, 학대하다 _____
3 정의를 내리다 _____
4 보급, 널리 퍼짐 _____
5 도입 _____
6 반응성 _____
7 측면 _____
8 ～로 구성되다 _____
9 줄이다 _____
10 수확(추수) _____
11 무시무시한 _____
12 종교적인 _____
13 복제 _____
14 도덕성, 윤리성 _____
15 실험(법) _____
16 진행 중인 _____
17 정복하다 _____
18 반대, 저항, 야당 _____
19 공중 납치하다 _____
20 그 후에 _____
21 기원 _____
22 희생자 _____
23 붕괴하다, 무너지다 _____
24 패배시키다 _____
25 ～을 방송하다 _____

B Translate into Korean.

1 treat _____
2 moral _____
3 meditation _____
4 worship _____
5 characteristic _____
6 guarantee _____
7 require _____
8 vital _____
9 placate _____
10 categorize _____
11 analysis _____
12 emphasis _____
13 conduct _____
14 infertile _____
15 fetus _____
16 ethical _____
17 plot _____
18 hardcore _____
19 due to _____
20 statement _____
21 numerous _____
22 deceased _____
23 be eager to _____
24 attempt to _____
25 mighty _____

Choose the correct answers to each question.

1 People have been debating the _____ of biological science and cloning.

① morality   ② collapse

③ fetus   ④ ongoing

2 There's a growing _____ for new housing in many rural areas.

① vital   ② need

③ unique   ④ categorize

3 Buddhists think that _____ and karma will lead them to Nirvana.

① Hinduism   ② mistreat

③ meditation   ④ force

D Translate into English or Korean.

1 He did a lot for this country, even though he committed serious errors.

2 In short, we want our children to develop a conscience - a powerful inner voice that will keep them on the right path.

3 그룹의 지도자는 생산적이고 긍정적인 결과를 얻기 위해서 이 교훈을 배워야 하며 이것을 실행으로 옮겨야 한다. (achieve, productive, positive, result)

Group leaders must learn this lesson and put it into practice _____ .

E Choose the correct words to fill in the blanks.

1 It's spring in Seoul, _____ it still feels like winter.

① so   ② therefore

③ even though   ④ for example

2 In the game, the players use a broomstick to throw an old bicycle tire _____ has been specially modified to make it floppy.

① it   ② those   ③ that   ④ this

3 In academic papers, you need to keep mentioning authors, pages, and dates to show _____ your ideas are related to those of the experts.

① what   ② how   ③ who   ④ which

F Choose the proper word for each sentence.

1 He was asked to [definite / define] his concept of cool.

2 It's too soon to give a [definite / define] answer.

3 Climate and weather affect every [aspect / inspect] of our lives.

4 Elaine went outside to [aspect / inspect] the playing field.

★ 명사절 접속사 that (that은 생략 가능)

They fear **(that)** these climbers may try to climb the biggest and tallest trees if they learn their exact locations.

그들은 이 나무 타는 사람들이 그것들의 정확한 위치를 알게 되면 가장 크고 가장 높은 나무들에 오르려고 할지도 모른다고 걱정한다.

★ 전치사의 목적어로 쓰이는 동명사

Music covers the whole range of emotions: it can make us feel happy or sad, helpless or energetic, and some music is capable **of** overtak**ing** the mind until we forget all else.

음악은 감정의 전 범위를 아우른다. 그것은 우리를 기쁘게 혹은 슬프게, 무기력하게 혹은 기운 넘치게 만들 수 있으며, 어떤 음악은 그밖의 모든 것을 우리가 잊을 때까지 정신을 압도할 수 있다.

★ anything but vs nothing but (결코[전혀] ~아닌 vs ~외에는, 단지 ~일 뿐)

Their plans for the village are **anything but** down-to-earth.

마을에 대한 그들의 계획은 결코 현실적인 것이 못된다.

I'm going to spend two weeks doing **nothing but** watching DVDs.

나는 2주 동안 아무것도 안 하고 DVD만 볼 것이다.

---

1 다음 문장에서 that이 생략된 부분을 찾으시오.

The boy sitting next to James said he could pass the exam because James had helped him a lot with the study.

2 다음 각 괄호 안에서 알맞은 것을 고르시오.

In my hometown, nobody would buy melon without [to feel / feeling] it and [to smell / smelling] it; and nobody would dream of [to buy / buying] chicken without [to know / knowing] which farm it came from and what it ate.

3 다음 우리말에 맞게 괄호 안에서 알맞은 것을 고르시오.

She has [anything / nothing] but a pretty face.
그녀는 예쁜 얼굴은 결코 아니다.

Daily Assignment Book

Homeroom teacher : _____

수업일		Contents (수업내용)	Homework (과제물)	Check (숙제검사)	
월	일			Done	Didn't do
월	일			Done	Didn't do
월	일			Done	Didn't do
나의 학습 아킬레스건	나의 취약 부분은?			Done	Didn't do
	해결 방법은?			Done	Didn't do
			Parent's Signature		

※ 학생들이 학원에서 공부한 내용입니다. 바쁘시더라도 관심을 갖고 확인해 주십시오.

어릴 적 Yo-Yo 하나면 있으면 세상을 다 가진 듯!

중국에서 시작된 것으로 추측되는 요요는 기원전 500년 경 그리스에서 어린이들이 나무나, 금속, 또는 테라코타 디스크로 만든 요요를 일정 나이가 되면 신에게 바쳤던 것으로 기록되어 있으며, 유카탄반도의 인류학 박물관에는 마야(서기 700년) 시대의 요요를 전시하고 있습니다. 요요는 약 2500년의 역사를 가진 장난감으로 두 번째로 오래되었다고 합니다. 실을 감았다 던졌다 당겼다 하면 바퀴가 실을 따라 돌며 위아래로 움직이는 장난감. 요요(Yo-Yo)는 사실 미국 Duncan 회사가 등록한 상품명입니다. 우리나라에도 수많은 인터넷 동호회가 있을 정도로 유명한 요요는 기네스북(Guinness Book of Records)에 실렸죠. 또 필리핀에서 요요는 400년 이상이나 무기로 사용되었고, 장난감으로서의 요요는 고대 그리스로 거슬러 올라갑니다. 고대 그리스인은 나무나 금속 등으로 만들고 신의 그림을 장식하기도 했습니다. 원래 필리핀 원주민들이 사냥할 때 쓰던 요요라는 말은 토속어로 '온다온다' 또는 '되돌아 온다'라는 의미를 가지고 있어요.

요요는 1960년대 이전에 이미 미국에 들어왔지만, 1965년 Duncan 회사가 상표로 등록하면서 본격적으로 생산에 들어갔습니다. Duncan 회사에서 내놓은 이 제품이 젊은이들 사이에서 열풍(Yo-Yo craze)을 일으키면서 그 후 다른 회사가 생산한 것도 모두 요요라고 부르게 되었죠. 요요가 오늘날까지도 꾸준히 끝없는 인기를 끌고 있는 이유는 다양합니다.

요요의 장점을 얘기하자면 요요는 양손을 사용하여 규칙적으로 꾸준하게 기술을 연습하면서 배워야 하므로 운동은 물론 집중력과 두뇌의 발달을 도와주고, 인내심과 자신감을 갖게 됩니다. 손의 여러 근육을 사용하므로 나이에 관계없이 사람들의 건강 놀이기구로 좋습니다. 또한 요요는 가격이 저렴하고 때가 되면 줄만 교체해 주면 오랫동안 사용할 수 있고, 휴대용으로 매우 적절하며 언제 어디서나 적당한 장소만 있으면 주머니에서 바로 꺼내 즐길 수 있는 놀이기구입니다.

MEMO

Bonus
Chapter

Bonus
Chapter

Unit 01 생각하는 대로!

Unit 02 인어공주를 봤어요!

Unit 03 하늘을 나는 포유류

Unit 04 장군! 왜군이 옵니다!

Unit 05 낮과 밤의 비밀

 단원 어휘

- [ ] **yell** v. 소리치다
- [ ] **examine** v. 검사(시험)하다
- [ ] **desperately** adv. 절망적으로, 필사적으로
- [ ] **scent** n. 냄새 v. 냄새를 풍기다
- [ ] **seduce** v. 유혹하다
- [ ] **supernatural** a. 초자연의, 신기의
- [ ] **foresee** v. 예견하다
- [ ] **assume** v. 가정하다, 추측하다
- [ ] **approximately** adv. 대략
- [ ] **comprise** v. ~으로 이루어지다
- [ ] **capable of** ~할 수 있는
- [ ] **orientation** n. 지향, 방위 측정
- [ ] **inhabit** v. 서식하다, 거주하다
- [ ] **misleading** a. 오도하는, 혼동케 하는
- [ ] **innocent** a. 순진한, 흠 없는
- [ ] **density** n. 밀도, 농도, 짙음
- [ ] **transmit** v. 전하다, 송신하다
- [ ] **axis** n. (회전체의) 축
- [ ] **represent** v. 나타내다, 표현하다
- [ ] **stick** v. 찌르다, 찔리다, 고집하다
- [ ] **slightly** adv. 약간

Mini Quiz Draw a line from each word on the left to its definition on the right. Then, use the numbered words to fill in the blanks in the sentences below.

1 yell

2 seduce

3 assume

4 approximately

5 axis

6 represent

a. to act on behalf of that person or group

b. the imaginary line around which a large round object, such as the Earth, turns

c. to think that something is true, although you do not have definite proof

d. to make you do something that you would not otherwise do.

e. close to the exact number, amount etc, but could be a little bit more or less than it

f. to shout or scream something, or speak in a very loud voice

7 Clare _____ in pain as she fell.

8 She was selected to _____ the company at the conference.

9 The plane will be landing in _____ 20 minutes.

10 The Earth rotates on a(n) _____ between the north and south poles.

11 I didn't see your car in front of your house, so I _____ you'd gone out.

12 The ads _____ people into spending money unnecessarily.

주어진 문장 넣기

한 단락은 시간적 구성 및 논리적 구성이 잘 짜여진 구조로 이루어져 있다. 주어진 문장이 지문 속의 어디에 놓여야 글의 통일성이 이루어지는지를 묻는 문제로, 글의 일관성에 의한 문장과 문장 간의 관계를 논리적으로 추론해야 한다. 전체적인 주제와 요지를 파악하고 글의 흐름이 시간적, 공간적으로 끊기거나 반전되는 부분을 찾아본다. 글을 읽으면서 두 문장 간의 흐름이 끊어지거나 연결이 어색한 곳을 찾아 주어진 문장을 넣어 글의 흐름이 자연스러우면 그 자리가 바로 정답이다.

문장 넣기 유형의 급소

❶ **주어진 문장의 앞뒤 내용을 추론해 보라.** 단락을 읽기 전, 주어진 문장을 꼼꼼하게 해석하여 그 앞뒤에 이어질 내용일 무엇일지 추론해 본다.

❷ **주어진 문장에 연결어가 사용된 경우 그 앞에 왔을 내용을 추론한다.** 주어진 문장에 연결어가 사용된 경우에는 그 앞의 내용을 추론한다. 예를 들어 however가 있는 경우에는 그 앞에는 주어진 내용과 반대되는 내용이 오고, therefore가 있으면 주어진 문장의 원인에 해당되는 문장이 앞에 오며, also는 앞에 주어진 문장과 유사한 내용이 와야 한다.

❸ **단락의 전개방식을 파악하라.** 비교-대조, 통념-비판, 문제-해결, 원인-결과, 진술-부연, 열거(나열) 등의 전개방식을 통해 추론할 수 있다. 예를 들어, 주어진 문장이 어떤 결과를 제시하고 있는 문장이라면, 그것은 어떤 원인이나 문제점이 제기된 문장 뒷부분들 중에 놓일 수 있기 때문이다.

❹ **대명사, 지시어, 연결어를 백분 활용하라.** 단락 내 가리키는 대상이 모호한 대명사나 지시어가 있다면 그 앞에 주어진 문장을 넣어 본다. 주어진 문장에 연결어가 있다면 이 연결어와 자연스럽게 연결될 수 있는 부분을 찾아본다.

❺ **주어진 문장을 넣어서 논리적인 비약이 없는지를 확인하라.** 연결어, 대명사, 지시어구, 부사, 관사, 시제의 흐름, 주어의 일관성 등, 단서가 될 만한 것들을 이용하여 주어진 문장이 들어갈 곳을 찾았다면 그 문장을 넣고 앞뒤 문장과의 논리적 어색함이 없는지 마지막으로 한 번 더 확인을 해야 한다.

글의 흐름상, 주어진 문장이 들어가기에 가장 적절한 곳은? 기출문제

Koreans tend to have one job for their whole life.

A professor of business studied employment patterns in Korea and the United States. (①) She described in her book some important differences. (②) Among them, she paid particular attention to the number of years a person stays with a job. (③) When they are young, they go to work for a company, and they stay with that company. (④) In the United States, people move from one company to another. (⑤) They changed jobs very frequently.

[논리독해]

Key-word : employment patterns (in Korea and the United States)

제시문의 핵심어 : Korean ~ have one job

수험생의 눈

▶ 첫 문장을 읽고 글의 전개방식을 파악한다.

▶ 한국인들은 일생동안 한 가지 직업에 종사하는 경향에 대한 구체적인 설명 바로 앞이 답이 된다.

▶ ④에서부터는 미국에 관한 내용이므로 ④번과 ⑤번에는 절대 들어갈 수 없다.

▶ ③ 뒤의 대명사 they는 누구를 대신하는지를 생각해 본다. 바로 한국인들을 지칭하는 말이다.

Psychology

Great thinkers and philosophers have disagreed on many matters, but they mostly agree on one point: "We become what we think about." Ralph Waldo Emerson once said, "A man is what he thinks about all day long." The Roman emperor Marcus Aurelius put it this way: "A man's life is what his thoughts make of it." In the Bible we find, "As a man thinks in his heart, so he is." One day, an old man was visiting his son's house. As he was taking a nap, his grandson put a piece of stinky-smelling cheese on his grandfather's mustache just as a joke. Soon, the grandfather awoke and yelled, "This room stinks." So he examined every room of the house in order to see **if** the other rooms smelled too. Every room smelled the same. So he left the house, but the stinky smell did not go away. Desperately, he yelled "the whole world stinks!" We are just like the old man when we have negative thoughts. Everything we experience and every person we see, carries the scent we hold in our mind.

1   **What is one thing that great thinkers and philosophers agree on?**

① They agree that we don't become what we think about.

② They agree that we become what we think about.

③ They agree that we want to be what we think about.

④ They agree that negativism fills our mind.

⑤ None of the above.

2   **What is this passage trying to explain?**

① We have to confirm everything before making any decisions.

② Bear in mind that thinkers and philosophers are always accurate.

③ It's very important to consider things.

④ We are guided by our minds.

⑤ Don't make fools of others, otherwise you will be paid back in the same way.

Check Your
VOCABULARY!

thinker	philosopher	emperor	put it this way
take a nap	stinky-smelling	mustache	yell
examine	go away	desperately	scent

동사 뒷자리에서 명사절 접속사로 쓰이는 if

▼ 동사 뒷자리

I think that websites should say if they are private or public.

내가 생각하기에 웹사이트들은 개인의 정보를 보호하는지 아니면 공개하는지를 밝혀야 한다.

▼ 동사 뒷자리

Please let me know if you agree to my plan.

당신이 제 계획에 동의하는지 아닌지 저에게 알려 주세요.

if가 이끄는 절은 문장 안에서 명사 자리에 들어가 명사 역할을 할 수 있기 때문에 명사절이라 한다. whether와 같은 의미로 '~인지 아닌지'로 해석한다. 현대 영어에서는 whether는 보통 문장 맨 앞에 쓰고, if는 보통 동사 표현 다음에 와서 목적어나 보어 역할을 한다.

동의하다 + ~인지 아닌지
➡ 동의하**는지 아닌지**
agree + if ➡ if + S + agree

if를 무조건 '만약 ~라면'으로 해석하면 안 된다. 영어는 정해진 특정 자리에서 그 뜻이 결정되므로 똑같이 생긴 if라 하더라도 동사 바로 뒷자리에 위치하면 그때의 if가 우리말 '~인지 아닌지'의 뜻을 나타낸다. 우리말은 단어 자체에 '~인지 아닌지'란 말을 붙여 만들 수 있지만 영어는 철저히 정해진 자리에서만 가능하다.

Practice

1 Certainly, Asians smile to try to be polite even when they are sad, but it is doubtful if such a behavior is unique to them.

해석 ◐ _____

2 소방관들이 the fire fighters 불이 the fire 지하실에서 났는지 아니면 부엌에서 났는지 started in the basement or the kitchen 몰랐다 did not know.

영작 ◐ _____

Super Speaking
1단계 : 처음 우리말과 영문을 보면서 영어로 말해본다.
2단계 : 영문을 손으로 가리고 우리말만 보면서 완전한 영어로 말할 수 있도록 3~4회 반복한다.

 그녀가 온다면 나도 갈 것이지만, 그녀가 올지 안 올지 나는 모른다.

I will come if she comes tomorrow, but I don't know if she will come.

우리말을 영 어 로 옮 기 기

 그들이 서로 좋아하는지 아닌지는 내게 중요하지 않다.

Whether they like each other or not isn't important to me.

 나는 그 비행기가 도착했는지 아닌지 모르겠다.

I don't know if the flight has arrived or not.

 나는 그들이 나에 대해 얘기하고 있었는지 아닌지를 알고 싶다.

I'd like to know if they were talking about me.

인어공주를 봤어요!

Mythical
Creature

In the sea, there live beautiful creatures named mermaids. A mermaid has an upper body which resembles that of a human female, but she has the tail of a fish instead of two legs. Mermaids live in a beautiful castle deep under the sea. Their beautiful faces and voices often seduce sailors who jump into the sea and eventually drown. _____, sometimes, they are kind enough to rescue sailors who fall into the water during storms. They also have supernatural powers to foresee the future.

Do mermaids actually exist? Are those fascinating stories about the mermaids real? Actually, mermaids are mythical creatures, just like unicorns and fairies which only exist in folklore and myths. Almost every culture has interesting stories about the origins of mermaids. In many cultures, it is believed that exhausted sailors saw a mirage or a sea creature in the distance and thought it had a human face. Since no human can survive in the sea, they assumed that it might have fins instead of legs.

1   **Choose the best answer to fill in the blank.**

① As a result   ② Similarly   ③ However

④ That is   ⑤ To begin with

2   이 글에서 밑줄 친 in the distance의 의미로 알맞은 것은?

① within approach   ② far away   ③ to a great extent

④ in a big space   ⑤ very close

Check Your
VOCABULARY!

mermaid	upper body	resemble	seduce
drown	supernatural	foresee	mythical
exhausted	mirage	assume	fin

enough to do

The pungsan dog of North Korea is a brave enough to fight with a tiger.
북한의 풍산개는 호랑이와 싸울 정도로 용감하다.

This book is easy enough for a ten-year old child to read.
이 책은 열 살 먹은 아이가 읽을 정도로 쉽다.

보통 enough 하면 거의 모든 학생들이 '충분히'의 뜻만을 알고 있다. 물론 enough가 명사를 단독으로 수식할 경우 '충분히'의 뜻이지만, to부정사와 함께 쓰일 때는 '~할 정도로'의 의미가 더 정확하다.

싸우다 + **~할 정도로** ➡ 싸울 **정도로**
fight + **enough to** ➡ **enough to** fight

to부정사가 enough 뒷자리에 있을 때 우리말 '~할 정도로'의 의미를 나타낸다. 의미상 주어(for + 명사)는 항상 부정사 바로 앞자리에 들어갈 수 있다. 이때의 의미상 주어는 우리말 '~가, ~는'처럼 주어의 뜻을 갖는다.

| Practice

1 After refining and improving the program, the computer engineers were confident enough to present it to Microsoft Corporation.

해석 ○ _____

2 Karen은 겨울 방학 동안 for winter vacation 그녀가 원한 모든 나라를 any country she wished 여행할 정도로 to tour 부자였다.

영작 ○ _____

| Super Speaking
1단계 : 처음 우리말과 영문을 보면서 영어로 말해본다.
2단계 : 영문을 손으로 가리고 우리말만 보면서 완전한 영어로 말할 수 있도록 3~4회 반복한다.

 그는 작은 요트로 혼자서 태평양을 건널 정도로 모험적이다.

He was adventurous enough to cross the Pacific in a small yacht by himself. 우리말을 영 어 로 옮 기 기

 Bob은 입학시험을 통과할 정도로 열심히 공부했다.

Bob studied hard enough to pass the entrance exam.

 그녀는 도둑을 쫓아갈 정도로 용감했다.

She was brave enough to run after the thief.

 그녀는 그 냉장고를 옮길 정도로 힘이 세다.

She is strong enough to carry the refrigerator.

Unit 03

하늘을 나는 포유류

Animal & Curious

In the world, there are at least 1,000 different species of bats. Bats are in the order Chiroptera. (a) Many of the world's bats live throughout the North American continent. (b) The United States is known to have approximately 44 species which comprise 15 genera of bats. Bats are the only mammals in the world capable of flying. (c) In addition, most species of bats have evolved a system of acoustic orientation, often referred to as 'bat radar.' The technical term for such a system is echolocation. Some bats, comprising 11 genera and more than 18 species, live in the southwestern deserts. (d) Most Big Free-tailed Bats, of which the common name is Mastiff Bats, inhabit the southern Sonoran and Chihuahuan deserts, but they are found on other continents, too. They are also known as Bulldog Bats because of their facial resemblance to bulldogs. (e) Bulldog bats eat insects that many people may consider pests. There are about 85 species of bats in the family.

1 **Which information does the passage mainly contain?**
① Explanation of bats' habitation
② Movements of bats
③ Description of species of bats, including Bulldog Bats
④ Bats' body structure
⑤ Protection of endangered species

2 (a)~(e) 중, 이 글의 흐름상 어색한 것은?
① (a)   ② (b)   ③ (c)   ④ (d)   ⑤ (e)

Check Your **VOCABULARY!**

order	Chiroptera	approximately	comprise
genera	mammal	capable of	evolve
acoustic	orientation	technical term	echolocation
inhabit	resemblance	habitation	endangered

there be 구문의 특징

There **is** an old deserted house on the top of the mountain.
산꼭대기에는 오래된 흉가가 하나 있다.

There **are** four suitcases sitting on the front porch.
4개의 가방이 앞쪽 현관에 놓여 있다.

be동사의 특징은 대표적으로 linking verb와 existence verb의 역할 두 가지로 나눌 수 있다. there와 함께 쓰일 때는 언제나 '존재'를 나타내게 된다. 이때 수의 일치 및 시제를 물어보는 문제로 구성할 수 있으니 정확히 이해해 두어야 한다. 특히 be동사 자리에 1형식 동사가 모두 들어갈 수 있다는 것도 유의해야 한다.

Practice

1 To some people, trying to talk over a cell phone in a foreign language seems difficult. There **is** a good reason for this difficulty.

해석 ◯ _____

2 한 쪽 양말만을 only one sock 신는 who wears 한 남자가 있다 a man.

영작 ◯ _____

Super Speaking   1단계 : 처음 우리말과 영문을 보면서 영어로 말해본다.
2단계 : 영문을 손으로 가리고 우리말만 보면서 완전한 영어로 말할 수 있도록 3~4회 반복한다.

    토의 안건 다음으로 여덟 가지 공지사항이 있습니다.

After the topics for discussion, there are 8 announcements.
우리말을
영어로
옮기기

    이 패밀리 레스토랑에 웬 사람들이 이렇게 많죠?

How come there are so many people in this family restaurant?

    영어 실력이 그와 맞먹는 자가 없다.

There is no one who can match him in his ability in English.

    전 세계에 많은 사람들이 생활보호를 필요로 한다.

There are a lot of people in the world who need welfare.

Unit 04 장군! 왜군이 옵니다!

Information Age

The claim that we have recently entered the information age is misleading. Flooded by (a) cellphones, the Internet, and television, we incorrectly imagine that our ancestors inhabited an innocent world where the news did not travel far beyond (b) the village. It may not be valid to (A) consume / assume that the media make our time distinct from the past, because we know relatively little about (B) how information was shared / how was information shared in the past. _____, the Olympics celebrate the memory of (c) the Greek soldier who brought the news of the Athenian victory over the Persians. Most of us could come up with many other examples — (d) message drums, smoke signals, church bells, ship flags. But their primitiveness would only confirm our sense that we live in a fundamentally different world, one of constant, instant access to information.

All ages have had a means of sharing information. What makes our time distinct is not the density of the data we take in. It is the technology that does the transmitting. Thanks to (e) satellites, we can find out instantly about events that occur on the other side of the world. It usually took five weeks for Benjamin Franklin in Paris to receive a letter sent from Philadelphia. But the news was still new and (C) surprised / surprising to people there. 기출

1 이 글의 요지로 가장 적절한 것은?

① The value of information depends on speed.

② We are entering a new age of information.

③ Even old information can benefit all of us.

④ Every age is in fact an age of information.

⑤ We are flooded by incorrect information.

2 (a)~(e) 중, 밑줄 친 <u>a means of sharing information</u>에 해당하지 <u>않는</u> 것은?

① (a)   ② (b)   ③ (c)

④ (d)   ⑤ (e)

3 Choose the correct answer that fits most appropriately in this passage.

	(A)	(B)	(C)
①	consume	... how information was shared ...	surprised
②	consume	... how was information shared ...	surprising
③	consume	... how information was shared ...	surprising
④	assume	... how information was shared ...	surprising
⑤	assume	... how was information shared ...	surprised

4 Choose the best answer to fill in the blank.

① Eventually

② However

③ In fact

④ Therefore

⑤ A few days later

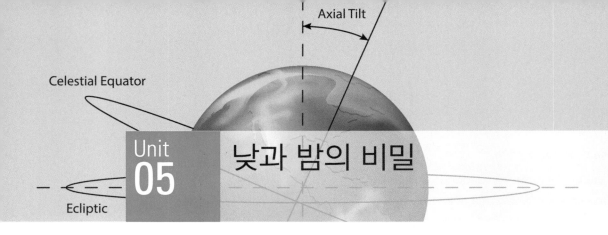

Axial Tilt

Celestial Equator

Ecliptic

Unit
05

낮과 밤의 비밀

Space
Science

Why do some countries have four seasons while some others have only one season? How do day and night change? As we know, the Earth circles around the Sun. Since _____, the distance between the Earth and the Sun is measured differently depending on where you are. When the Earth is on the left side of the Sun, the northern hemisphere is farther from the Sun than the southern hemisphere; when the Earth is on the right side of the Sun, the southern hemisphere is farther from the Sun than the northern hemisphere. Thus, when summer occurs in the northern hemisphere, people in the southern hemisphere have winter.

While the seasonal changes are caused by the Earth's orbiting motion around the Sun, the rotation of the Earth on its own axis gives us day and night. In order to better understand, let's do a simple scientific experiment. First, you need to prepare a lamp, an apple and a knitting needle. If you are ready, put the lamp in the middle of the room. The lamp represents the Sun and the apple represents the Earth. Now stick the knitting needle in the apple so that the needle represents the axis of the Earth.

Now spin the knitting needle so that the apple can spin on the needle. It shows how the Earth rotates on its axis. The Earth spins on its axis every day, which lets most of the Earth have sunlight for a certain amount of time everyday. While one side of the Earth has sunlight, the other side cannot receive any. That is why longitudinal difference causes a time difference. However, remember that the axis of the Earth is tilted slightly. If you circle the apple around the lamp while letting the needle lean to one side at an angle of 23.5° from the perpendicular, you will be able to notice that at one side of the room the lamp keeps shining on the top of the apple, while the bottom of the apple remains in darkness continuously; and vice versa at the other side of the room. Thus, if you are at one of the poles, you will be in total darkness for half of the year, but in continuous daylight for the other half of the year.

1　**Choose the most suitable answer to fill in the blank.**

① the Earth has been created by something

② we can't measure the exact distance

③ the Sun is hot enough to push the Earth

④ the axis of the Earth is slightly tilted

⑤ the circulation of the Earth is irregular

2　**Choose the reason why we have days and nights.**

① the revolving around the Sun

② the rotation of the Earth on its axis

③ the lunar eclipse

④ the solar eclipse

⑤ the Earth's orbit

3　**What could happen if the axis of the earth was not tilted?**

① There would only be two seasons year-round.

② Seasons would change irregularly.

③ The temperature would be about 23°C most of the time.

④ The Earth would rotate faster.

⑤ The northern hemisphere and the southern hemisphere could have the same seasons.

4　**What is this passage trying to explain?**

① Clarifying the difference between the northern hemisphere and the southern hemisphere

② Importance of the Sun and how it affects us

③ How to prepare for an experiment on the Earth's rotation

④ How to prepare for an experiment on the Earth briefly

⑤ The repetition of day and night, and why there are four seasons

Check Your VOCABULARY!

circle around

measure

depending on

northern hemisphere

southern hemisphere

seasonal

orbiting motion

rotation

axis

knitting needle

represent

stick

spin

longitudinal

tilt

slightly

lean

angle

perpendicular

continuously

vice versa

circulation

lunar eclipse

solar eclipse

briefly

WORD REVIEW

A Translate into English.

1 철학자 _____

2 소리치다 _____

3 낮잠 자다 _____

4 콧수염 _____

5 사라지다 _____

6 필사적으로, 절망적으로 _____

7 예견하다 _____

8 가정하다 _____

9 익사하다 _____

10 오도하는 _____

11 전문 용어 _____

12 기진맥진한, 지친 _____

13 범람하다, 가득 차다 _____

14 조상 _____

15 근본적으로 _____

16 즉각적으로 _____

17 기울다 _____

18 계절에 따른 _____

19 경도의 _____

20 반대로, 거꾸로 _____

21 밀도 _____

22 ~덕분에 _____

23 (회전체의) 축 _____

24 ~을 넘어서서 _____

25 순진한, 단순한 _____

B Translate into Korean.

1 resemble _____

2 capable of _____

3 endangered _____

4 examine _____

5 approximately _____

6 upper body _____

7 seduce _____

8 comprise _____

9 supernatural _____

10 acoustic _____

11 resemblance _____

12 inhabit _____

13 distinct _____

14 constant _____

15 primitiveness _____

16 satellite _____

17 orbiting motion _____

18 rotation _____

19 represent _____

20 circle around _____

21 valid _____

22 come up with _____

23 transmit _____

24 continuously _____

25 lean _____

Choose the correct answers to each question.

1 In the world, there are at least 1,000 different _____ of bats.

① species ② mammals

③ inhabit ④ resemblance

2 Bats are the only _____ in the world capable of flying.

① genera ② orientation

③ habitation ④ mammals

3 The _____ changes are caused by the Earth's orbit around the Sun.

① perpendicular ② rotation

③ longitudinal ④ seasonal

D **Translate into English or Korean.**

1 An increasing number of elderly people in Japan are deciding that they are still young enough to keep working.

_____

_____

2 When they send their children to a sports camp, parents should talk with the sports coaches to see if they will respect the children's wishes.

_____

_____

3 우리가 영어를 공부해야 하는 몇 가지 이유들이 있다. (several reasons, why)

_____ we should study English.

E **Choose the correct words to fill in the blanks.**

1 Can you tell me _____ she has any experience in the staging field at all?

① if ② so ③ and ④ but

2 Engineers make skyscrapers _____ to withstand earthquakes, high wind, and severe changes in temperature.

① strong enough ② enough strong

③ too strong ④ so strong

3 _____ nothing better than a fresh roasted head of garlic with a warm loaf of French bread for breakfast.

① This is ② These are

③ There is ④ There are

F **Choose the proper word for each sentence.**

1 The system [transforms / transmits] information over digital phone lines.

2 The fairy [transformed / transmitted] the pumpkin into a carriage.

3 We should [assume / consume] less fossil fuels.

4 I [assume / consume] that the plan will bring a good result.

SENTENCE REVIEW

Darwin was the first to propose that long necks evolved in giraffes **because** *they enabled* the animals to eat the treetop leaves.

다윈은 기린들의 목이 길게 진화한 것이 나무의 윗부분에 있는 잎들을 먹을 수 있도록 하기 위해서라고 제안한 최초의 사람이었다.

★ being이 생략된 분사구문

(*Being*) **Situated** at an elevation of 1,350m, the city of Kathmandu, which looks out on the sparkling Himalayas, enjoys a warm climate year-round that makes living here pleasant.

해발 1,350미터에 위치하고 있으면서, 반짝이는 히말라야 산맥이 내다보이는 카트만두시는 일 년 내내 살기 좋은 온화한 기후이다.

★ [part / some / all / most / half / a lot / the rest / 비율 / 분수] + of + 명사
  → 명사에 따라 단수 or 복수 결정

Some of *the information* **needs** to be downloaded to be opened.

몇몇 정보는 열어보려면 다운로드를 받아야 한다.

Most of *English learners* **want** to know the differences between British and American English.

대부분의 영어를 배우는 사람들은 영국영어와 미국영어의 차이점을 알고 싶어 한다.

---

1 다음 문장에서 틀린 부분을 찾아 바르게 고치시오.

We study philosophy because the mental skills it helps us develop.

➡ _____

2 다음 괄호 안에서 알맞은 것을 고르시오.

They all reached the beach two hours late, [exhausting / exhausted] but safe.

3 다음 괄호 안에서 알맞은 것을 고르시오.

Nearly half of Tajikistan's population [is / are] under 14 years of age.

Daily Assignment Book

Homeroom teacher : _____

수업일	Contents (수업내용)	Homework (과제물)	Check (숙제검사)	
월 일			Done	Didn't do
월 일			Done	Didn't do
월 일			Done	Didn't do
나의 학습 아킬레스건	나의 취약 부분은?		Done	Didn't do
	해결 방법은?		Done	Didn't do
		Parent's Signature		

※ 학생들이 학원에서 공부한 내용입니다. 바쁘시더라도 관심을 갖고 확인해 주십시오.

아시아 최고의 프리미어리거! 박지성!

박지성은 서울에서 태어나 수원에서 자랐습니다. 박지성은 가난한 집안에서 태어났다고 합니다. 정육점을 하셨던 아버지는 집안 형편이 그리 좋지 못해서 좋은 축구화 하나 못 사주셨다고 합니다. 어려서부터 축구에 대한 대단한 열정 때문에 부모님께 몹시 졸라서 산남초등학교 축구부에 들어갔답니다. 하지만 그 축구부는 1년 이상 지속되지 못하고 폐부되어 박지성에게 실망을 안겨줍니다. 그 후 박지성은 세류초등학교로 전학을 가게 됩니다. 6학년 때 쯤에 박지성은 차범근 어린이 축구상을 받았습니다. 그리고 중학생이 되어서 안용중학교에서 축구부 활동을 계속했습니다. 안용중학교는 그다지 축구로 잘 알려지지 않은 학교였는데 박지성 선수가 안용중학교 축구부를 상위권 팀으로 끌어올렸다고 합니다. 그 후 수원공업고등학교 들어갑니다. 박지성은 당시 감독님께 많은 것을 배웠다고 합니다. 고등학교를 마친 후 박지성은 체격조건이 맞지 않아 거절당하던 중 명지대 축구부의 빈자리를 메꿀 수 있는 기회가 옵니다. 결국 대학교 축구부에 간신히 들어간 박지성은 열성적인 태도와 그의 숨은 잠재력을 발휘해 일본 J-리그의 시미즈 에스펄스에서 이적 제의가 들어왔으나 연봉협상에서 문제가 생겨 결국 결렬됩니다. 그리고 그다음 교토 퍼플상가에서 이적제의가 들어옵니다. 박지성은 그리하여 일본 J-리그로 진출합니다. 올림픽 선수로 뛰고, 일본 J리거로 뛰다가 2002 월드컵, 박지성이 날개를 달게 됩니다. 히딩크 감독은 박지성이 잠재력이 아주 많은 가능성 있는 선수라고 판단하고 그를 월드컵 예선, 본선 경기들에 꾸준히 출전시킵니다. 월드컵이 끝난 후 히딩크는 박지성을 스카웃해 PSV 아인트호벤에서 뛰게 합니다. 박지성은 PSV의 핵심선수가 되면서 그의 활약을 본 유럽의 여러 팀들이 박지성에 대해 관심을 갖기 시작했습니다. 그 후 유럽의 여러 명문팀에서 박지성을 영입하려고 시도했습니다. 대표적으로 토트넘, 리버풀, 첼시, 맨유 등으로 이러한 엄청난 팀들이었습니다. 결국 박지성은 첼시에서 내건 천만 파운드보다 좀 적은 500만~700만 파운드 정도의 금액으로 맨유행을 결정합니다. 박지성은 떠나면서 자신을 키워준 히딩크에 대한 감사의 표시로 이적료 중 10%를 PSV 아인트호벤의 유소년 축구에 기부합니다. 그리고 맨유에 도착한 박지성은 같은 PSV 출신인 루드 반 니스텔루이와 친하게 지냅니다. 같은 PSV 출신이라서 박지성 선수에게 아주 잘해 주었습니다. 박지성 선수와 반니스텔루이는 같이 자주 어울리는 그런 아주 친한 친구 사이였습니다. 박지성은 또 루니, 에브라, 반데사르, 네빌, 스콜스, 호나우두, 사하, 긱스, 실베스트르 같은 스타플레이어들과도 아주 친해졌습니다. 맨유 구단 사람들도 박지성의 친근하고 예의 있는 인간성 때문에 그를 아주 좋아한다고 합니다.

WORD LIST • Chapter 01

1	**huge**	거대한	26	**surface**	수면, 표면
2	**ancient**	고대의	27	**used to do**	~하곤 했다
3	**zoologist**	동물학자	28	**mammal**	포유동물
4	**ancestor**	조상	29	**gill**	아가미
5	**conflict**	갈등, 분쟁	30	**a majority of**	대다수의
6	**political**	정치(학)의	31	**regardless of**	~와 관계없이
7	**politician**	정치인	32	**struggle**	분투하다, 싸움
8	**prosecutor**	검사, 검찰관	33	**reflect**	~을 반영하다, 반사하다
9	**block**	막다, 차단하다	34	**insulation**	단열재, 절연체
10	**Arctic**	북극	35	**palm tree**	야자나무
11	**fibrous**	섬유의, 섬유가 많은	36	**access to**	~에 접근
12	**durability**	내구성(력)	37	**solar radiation**	태양 복사열
13	**aircar**	비행선	38	**clatter**	덜커덕거리다
14	**orbit**	범위, 궤도	39	**duration**	지속
15	**altitude**	고도	40	**incredible**	믿을 수 없는, 놀라운
16	**long for**	동경하다	41	**of use**	쓸모 있는
17	**stick to**	~를 고수하다, 얽매이다	42	**adjustment**	조절, 조정
18	**under control**	감독 하에, 지시 하에	43	**ease**	속도를 늦추다, 완화하다
19	**supervise**	감독하다, 관리하다	44	**land**	(~에) 착륙하다
20	**fit (into)**	~에 적합하다	45	**procedure**	절차, 행위, 조치
21	**evolve**	진화하다	46	**disturbingly**	방해가 되게
22	**annoying**	짜증나게 하는	47	**irresistible**	억누를 수 없는
23	**fertile region**	비옥한 지역	48	**urge**	충동
24	**available**	이용 가능한	49	**attentive**	주의 깊은
25	**undertake**	(일을) 맡다, 책임지다	50	**objective**	목표

WORD LIST • Chapter 02

1	label	꼬리표
2	advertise	광고하다, 선전하다
3	detergent	세제, 세제
4	get over	～에서 회복하다
5	depressed	우울한
6	tend to	～하는 경향이 있다
7	negative feeling	부정적인 감정
8	be willing to	기꺼이 ～하다
9	indoors	실내에서
10	consonant	자음
11	vocabulary	어휘, 단어
12	talent	재능
13	well-known	잘 알려진
14	acknowledged	인정받은
15	regret	후회하다
16	fame	평판, 명성
17	screw up	망치다
18	concern	걱정
19	awful	몹시 나쁜
20	appetite	식욕
21	tempt	마음을 끌다, 유혹하다
22	master	숙달하다
23	gradually	점진적으로
24	pretend to	～인 체하다
25	as if	마치 ～처럼

26	awesome	굉장한, 아주 멋진
27	content	내용물
28	stomachache	복통, 위통
29	as a matter of fact	사실은, 실제로
30	liquid	액체
31	influence	영향
32	in contrast	대조적으로
33	as usual	평상시대로
34	seem like	～처럼 보이다
35	articulate	똑똑히 발음하다
36	lighten	기운나게 하다
37	affect	영향을 미치다
38	pronunciation	발음, 발음법
39	overconfident	지나치게 자신감 있는
40	possibility	가능성
41	penniless	무일푼의, 빈털털이의
42	deceive	속이다
43	never mind	괜찮다, 걱정하지 마라
44	a couple of shots	두서너 대의 주사
45	stomach cramp	위경련
46	totally	완전히, 총체적으로
47	on the contrary	반대로
48	frequently	자주, 여러 번
49	for one's sake	～을 위하여
50	expression	표정

WORD LIST • Chapter 03

1	**thinker**	사상가, 사색가
2	**ruler**	통치자, 지배자
3	**Confucianism**	유교
4	**poverty**	빈곤, 가난
5	**advertisement**	광고
6	**manufacturer**	제조업자
7	**intend to**	~할 의도이다
8	**exclusively**	오로지, 독점적으로
9	**obey**	복종하다, 응하다
10	**necessarily**	부득이, 할 수 없이
11	**composer**	작곡가
12	**satisfaction**	만족(감)
13	**temperature**	온도, 기온
14	**deforest**	벌채하다
15	**current rate**	현재 비율
16	**alternative energy**	대체 에너지
17	**keeper**	관리자
18	**isolate**	고립시키다
19	**humane act**	인도적 행위
20	**set out**	시작하다, 착수하다
21	**relatively**	비교적, 상대적으로
22	**means**	수단, 방법
23	**carbon dioxide**	이산화탄소
24	**replace**	대체하다, 교체하다
25	**courageous**	용기 있는

26	**dutiful**	성실한, 충실한
27	**prudent**	신중한, 분별 있는
28	**considerate**	사려 깊은
29	**devote**	헌신하다
30	**product**	제품, 상품
31	**cost-effective**	비용 효율이 높은
32	**be likely to**	~할 것 같다
33	**inform**	알리다
34	**explore**	탐험하다
35	**mention**	~에 대해 언급하다
36	**release**	방출하다
37	**consequently**	결과적으로
38	**iceberg**	빙산
39	**fossil fuel**	화석 연료
40	**cut down**	축소하다, 줄어들다
41	**rescue**	구조하다, 구조
42	**lighthouse**	등대
43	**terrify**	무섭게 하다
44	**worn out**	기진맥진한
45	**along with**	~와 함께, 더불어
46	**guarantee**	보장
47	**emission**	방출
48	**blame for**	~에 대해 비난하다
49	**expanding**	확장하는, 팽창하는
50	**against**	~에 반대하여

1	Buddhist	불교도	26	treat	대우하다, 음식
2	mistreat	혹사하다, 학대하다	27	moral	도덕적인
3	define	정의를 내리다	28	meditation	명상
4	prevalence	보급, 널리 퍼짐	29	worship	숭배하다
5	introduction	도입	30	characteristic	특성, 특징
6	responsiveness	반응성	31	guarantee	보증하다
7	aspect	측면	32	require	~을 필요로 하다
8	be composed of	~로 구성되다	33	vital	중요한
9	shorten	줄이다	34	placate	달래다, 위로하다
10	harvest	수확(추수)	35	categorize	범주화하다
11	spooky	무시무시한	36	analysis	분석
12	religious	종교적인	37	emphasis	강조
13	cloning	복제	38	conduct	수행하다, 실시하다
14	morality	도덕성, 윤리성	39	infertile	생식력이 없는
15	experimentation	실험(법)	40	fetus	태아
16	ongoing	진행 중인	41	ethical	윤리적인
17	subdue	정복하다	42	plot	음모를 꾸미다
18	opposition	반대, 저항, 야당	43	hardcore	단호한, 강경한
19	hijack	공중 납치하다	44	due to	~ 때문에
20	subsequently	그 후에	45	statement	연설, 주장
21	origin	기원	46	numerous	수많은, 다수의
22	victim	희생자	47	deceased	죽은
23	collapse	붕괴하다, 무너지다	48	be eager to	~에 열심이다
24	defeat	패배시키다	49	attempt to	~하기를 시도하다
25	broadcast	~을 방송하다	50	mighty	강력한

WORD LIST • Bonus Chapter

1	philosopher	철학자		26	resemble	~을(와) 닮다
2	yell	소리치다		27	capable of	~할 수 있는
3	take a nap	낮잠 자다		28	endangered	멸종 위기에 처한
4	mustache	콧수염		29	examine	살펴보다, 검사하다
5	go away	사라지다		30	approximately	대략
6	desperately	필사적으로, 절망적으로		31	upper body	상반신
7	foresee	예견하다		32	seduce	유혹하다, 꼬드기다
8	assume	가정하다		33	comprise	~으로 이루어지다
9	drown	익사하다		34	supernatural	초자연적인
10	misleading	오도하는		35	acoustic	청각의
11	technical term	전문 용어		36	resemblance	비슷함
12	exhausted	기진맥진한, 지친		37	inhabit	서식하다
13	flood	범람하다, 가득 차다		38	distinct	다른, 별개의
14	ancestor	조상		39	constant	끊임없는
15	fundamentally	근본적으로		40	primitiveness	원시성, 원시적인 것
16	instantly	즉각적으로		41	satellite	인공위성
17	tilt	기울다		42	orbiting motion	공전운동
18	seasonal	계절에 따른		43	rotation	회전, 순환
19	longitudinal	경도의		44	represent	상징하다, 나타내다
20	vice versa	반대로, 거꾸로		45	circle around	주변을 돌다
21	density	밀도		46	valid	타당한
22	thanks to	~덕분에		47	come up with	떠오르다
23	axis	(회전체의) 축		48	transmit	전하다, 전송하다
24	beyond	~을 넘어서서		49	continuously	지속적으로
25	innocent	순진한, 단순한		50	lean	기대다

Answer Key

Chapter 01

Mini Quiz
p.14

1	e	7	evolved
2	c	8	huge
3	d	9	orbit
4	a	10	available
5	f	11	landed
6	b	12	attentive

Reading Skill
p.15

④ (C) – (A) – (B)

Unit 01
p.16

1 ④   **2** ②

huge	거대한	full-grown	충분히 성장한
mammal	포유동물	warm-blooded animal	온혈동물
womb	자궁	gill	아가미
surface	수면	zoologist	동물학자
ancestor	조상	used to do	~하곤 했(었)다
ancient	고대의	evolve	진화하다, 발전하다

Writing & Speaking
p.17

1 우리 사회에서 가장 많이 교육받은 대다수의 사람들이 우리나라의 역사를 거의 모른다는 것은 매우 놀라운 일이다.
2 It is not clear that God created the whole world.

Unit 02
p.18

1 ③   **2** ①

conflict	갈등	political	정치(학)의
struggle	싸움, 다툼	politician	정치가
prosecutor	검사, 검찰관	a majority of	대다수의
regardless of	~와 관계없이	annoying	짜증나게 하는
disturbingly	방해가 되게	lousy	많이 있는, 엉망인
disturb	방해하다	reflect	~을 반영하다

Writing & Speaking
p.19

1 그 학생은 다리가 짧고 강하지 않기 때문에 우수한 축구 선수가 되는 것은 어렵다. 그 결과, 그는 골프와 탁구를 배우고 있다.
2 It is wrong to give children everything they want.

Unit 03
p.20

1 ②   **2** ③

fertile region	비옥한 지역	available	이용 가능한, 쓸모 있는
block	블록, 막다, 차단하다	solar radiation	태양 복사열
insulation	단열재, 절연체	durability	내구성(력)

Arctic	북극	access to	~에 접근
be made of	~로 만들어지다	bamboo	대나무
palm tree	야자나무	fibrous	섬유의, 섬유질의

Writing & Speaking
p.21

1 그들은 서로 도와주고, 일에 자부심을 느끼며, 유쾌한 작업환경 유지를 조성하는 직원을 찾는다.
2 A person who has faith in himself can be faithful to others.

Unit 04
p.22

1 ④   **3** ③
2 ④   **4** ⑤

rooftop	지붕 위의	of use	쓸모 있는
aircar	비행선	ease	속도를 늦추다
swing	흔들리다	crash	요란한 소리를 내다
incredible	믿을 수 없는, 놀라운	violence	격렬함, 폭력
boom	울리다	roar	으르렁거리다
long-range	장거리의	altitude	고도
bang	쾅 소리를 내다	clatter	덜커덕거리다
smooth	부드러운	orbit	범위, 궤도
long for	동경하다	all of a sudden	갑자기
irresistible	억누를 수 없는	urge	충동
duration	지속	appeal to	~에 호소하다
power up	동력을 증가시키다	lift	끌어올리다
deck	갑판		

Unit 05
p.24

1 ①   **3** ①
2 ⑤   **4** ②

stick to	~을 고수하다, 얽매이다	emergency situation	응급상황
overly	과도하게, 지나치게	attentive	세심한, 주의 깊은
procedure	절차, 행위, 조치	supervise	감독하다, 관리하다
ignore	무시하다	under control	지시(감독) 하에
otherwise	그렇지 않으면	at risk	위험에 처한
land	착륙하다	priority	우선순위
struggle	분투하다, 싸움	cost	희생
objective	목표	in order to	~하기 위하여
fit (into)	~에 적합하다	lose sight of	~을 잃다, 안 보이다
exactly	정확히	route	항로, 진로
adjustment	조절, 조정	achieve	달성하다, 성취하다
judge	판단하다	undertake	(일을) 맡다, 책임지다
overlook	간과하다	composure	침착함
meticulous	신중한, 주의 깊은		

WORD REVIEW
p.26

A

1	huge	14	orbit
2	ancient	15	altitude
3	zoologist	16	long for
4	ancestor	17	stick to
5	conflict	18	under control
6	political	19	supervise
7	politician	20	fit (into)
8	prosecutor	21	evolve

9	block	22	annoying
10	Arctic	23	fertile region
11	fibrous	24	available
12	durability	25	undertake
13	aircar		

B	1	수면, 표면	14	지속
	2	~하곤 했다	15	믿을 수 없는, 놀라운
	3	포유동물	16	쓸모 있는
	4	아가미	17	조절, 조정
	5	대다수의	18	속도를 늦추다, 완화하다
	6	~와 관계없이	19	(~에) 착륙하다
	7	분투하다, 싸움	20	절차, 행위, 조치
	8	~을 반영하다, 반사하다	21	방해가 되게
	9	단열재, 절연체	22	억누를 수 없는
	10	야자나무	23	충동
	11	~에 접근	24	주의 깊은
	12	태양 복사열	25	목표
	13	덜커덕거리다		

C	1	②	3	③
	2	④		

D	1	아무도 나서서 그 할머니를 도와주려 하지 않았다는 사실은 놀라웠다.
	2	그는 2010년에 전쟁이 일어나는 것뿐만 아니라 누가 이길 것인지도 예언했다.
	3	people ask questions, other people who know the answers explain them

E	1	④	3	②
	2	①	4	③

F	1	d, h	4	b, j
	2	a, f	5	e, g
	3	c, i		

SENTENCE REVIEW p.28

1	appear	3	others see you
2	③ on → at		→ how others see you

Chapter 02

Mini Quiz p.30

1	d	7	detergent
2	b	8	pretend

3	e	9	regretted
4	a	10	vocabulary
5	f	11	expression
6	c	12	lighten

Reading Skill p.31
③ 병원에서 간호보조원으로 일했다.

Unit 01 p.32
1 ③   2 ①

mailbox	(개인의) 우편함	label	꼬리표, 라벨
awesome	굉장한, 아주 멋진	hopefully	바라건대
content	내용(물)	stomachache	복통, 위통
as a matter of fact	사실은, 실제로	soap	비누
liquid	액체	detergent	세정제, 세제
advertise	광고하다, 선전하다	get over	~에서 회복하다

Writing & Speaking p.33
1 많은 과학자들이 지구가 무언가에 의해 창조되었다고 믿는다.
2 Most college students know good jobs are hard to find.

Unit 02 p.34
1 ②   2 ④

seem	~처럼 보이다	influence	영향
gloomy	우울한, 침울한	depressed	우울한
negative feeling	부정적인 감정	indoors	실내에서
in contrast	대조적으로	lighten	기운 나게 하다, 기쁘게 하다
tend to do	~하는 경향이 있다	friendly	친절한
be willing to	기꺼이 ~하다	affect	~에 영향을 끼치다

Writing & Speaking p.35
1 연구는 나이가 신체 상태보다는 정신 상태라는 일반적인 지혜를 확인시켜 준다.
2 The old man always thanked God for the fact that he was still alive.

Unit 03 p.36
1 ⑤   2 ⑤

seem like	~처럼 보이다	totally	완전히, 총체적으로
pronunciation	발음	tend to	~하는 경향이 있다
consonant	자음	certain	어떤
on the contrary	반대로	articulate	똑똑히(또렷하게) 발음하다
vocabulary	어휘, 단어	name	말하다, 명명하다
lorry	대형 트럭	bonnet	덮개, 커버

Writing & Speaking p.37
1 부모들은 자녀들의 교우관계가 이루어지는 무대를 마련한다.
2 My girlfriend always bought me presents which were cheap.

Unit 04 p.38
1 ②   3 ①

2 ①		4 ⑤	
talent	재능	tempt	마음을 끌다, 유혹하다
fame	평판, 명성	professor	교수
well-known	유명한, 잘 알려진	acknowledged	인정받은
master	숙달하다	possibility	가능성
make a mistake	실수하다	be sure	확신하다
quickly	빨리	overconfident	지나치게 자신을 가지는
frequently	자주, 여러 번	for one's sake	~을 위하여
quit	멈추다, 그만 두다	ignore	무시하다
gradually	점진적으로	penniless	빈털터리의, 무일푼의
regret	후회하다	seriously	진지하게
degree	학위	make a living	생계를 꾸리다

11	기운나게 하다	24	~을 위하여
12	영향을 미치다	25	표정
13	발음, 발음법		

C	1	①	3	①
	2	②		

D
1 아이들은 수영장에 근무하고 있는 응급 구조대가 없는 것을 걱정했다.
2 그들은 크리스마스 전에 그들의 부모님으로부터 무엇을 받을지를 알고 싶어 한다.
3 which enable them to make good use of

E	1	②	3	③
	2	③	4	①

F	1	b, g	4	h, j
	2	d, i	5	c, f
	3	a, e		

Unit 05 p.40

1 ②		3 ④	
2 ③		4 ③	
screw up	망치다	be punished	벌 받다
would rather	차라리 ~하겠다	allow	허락하다
miss	(학교, 수업 등을) 빠지다	pretend to	~인 체하다
as usual	평상시대로	wry	얼굴을 찡그린
as if	마치 ~처럼	stomach cramp	위경련
concern	걱정	deceive	속이다
expression	표정, (얼굴의) 안색	awful	몹시 나쁜
appetite	식욕	at least	적어도, 최소한
effective	효과적인	a couple of shots	두서너 대의 주사
immediately	즉시, 바로	never mind	괜찮다, 걱정하지 마라
indifferent	무관심한	exhausted	지친, 기진맥진한
logical	논리적인	trick	속이다, 잔꾀
injection	주사	fool	속이다

SENTENCE REVIEW p.44

1	③	3	which
2	would have seen		

WORD REVIEW p.42

A
1	label	14	acknowledged
2	advertise	15	regret
3	detergent	16	fame
4	get over	17	screw up
5	depressed	18	concern
6	tend to	19	awful
7	negative feeling	20	appetite
8	be willing to	21	tempt
9	indoors	22	master
10	consonant	23	gradually
11	vocabulary	24	pretend to
12	talent	25	as if
13	well-known		

B
1	광장한, 아주 멋진	14	지나치게 자신감 있는
2	내용물	15	가능성
3	복통, 위통	16	무일푼의, 빈털털이의
4	사실은, 실제로	17	속이다
5	액체	18	괜찮다, 걱정하지 마라
6	영향	19	두서너 대의 주사
7	대조적으로	20	위경련
8	평상시대로	21	완전히, 총체적으로
9	~처럼 보이다	22	반대로
10	똑똑히 발음하다	23	자주, 여러 번

Chapter 03

Mini Quiz p.46

1	b	7	satisfaction
2	d	8	immediately
3	f	9	intend to
4	a	10	courageous
5	c	11	ruler
6	e	12	consequently

Reading Skill p.47

③ 이 때문에, 개미는 땅 밖으로 나와서 그 유충을 공격한다.

Unit 01 p.48

1 ③		2 ③	
Confucius	공자	thinker	사상가, 사색가
suffer from	~로부터 고통을 겪다	poverty	빈곤, 가난
dutiful	성실한, 충실한	obedient	순종하는
prudent	신중한, 분별 있는	studious	학문을 좋아하는

| considerate | 사려 깊은 | obey | 따르다, 응하다, 복종하다 |
| mature | 분별 있는, 성숙한 | Confucianism | 유교 |

1 Vicky는, 두꺼운 겨울 외투를 입고 있는데, 내일의 연극 발표회를 위해서 무대에서 연습을 하고 있다.

2 The girl liked the ghost, who played with her.

Unit 02 p.50

1 ③　　**2** ②

advertisement	광고(= ad)	guarantee	보장
fixed	고정된	advertiser	광고주
exclusively	오로지, 독점적으로	be likely to	~할 것 같다
product	제품, 상품	relatively	비교적, 상대적으로
inform	(~에 관하여) 알리다	cost-effective	비용 효율이 높은
manufacturer	제조업자	intend to	~할 의도이다

1 우리 선생님은 우리에게 그것을 5번씩 다시 쓰게 하셨다.

2 I will have Mark fix my bicycle.

Unit 03 p.52

1 ①　　**2** ⑤

necessarily	부득이, 할 수 없이	material value	물질적인 가치
self-satisfaction	자기만족	composer	작곡가
devote	헌신하다, 바치다	ordinary	평범한, 보통의
achieve	성취하다, 획득하다	explore	탐험하다
mention	~에 대하여 언급하다	excitement	흥미, 즐거움
means	수단, 방법	amusement	즐거움

1 그들 자신의 역사와 세계의 역사를 이해하는 사람들은 미래에 일어날 일을 예상하는 것이 더 쉬울 것이다.

2 Those who don't help others won't be helped by others.

Unit 04 p.54

1 ④　　**3** ①
2 ②　　**4** ③

temperature	온도, 기온	carbon dioxide	이산화탄소
atmosphere	대기	release	방출하다
iceberg	빙산	melt	녹다
consequently	결과적으로	in other words	다시 말해서
reduce	줄이다, 감소시키다	emission	방사, 방출
alternative energy	대체 에너지	solar power	태양력
replace	대체하다, 교체하다	fossil fuel	화석 연료
acre	에이커 (약 1,224평)	tropical forest	열대우림
cut down	축소하다, 줄어들다	deforest	벌채하다
cattle ranching	가축 방목	provide A with B	A에게 B를 제공하다
expanding	확장하는, 팽창하는	blame for	~에 대해 비난하다
be gone	사라지다	deforestation	산림 벌채, 산림 개간
current rate	현재 비율		

Unit 05 p.56

1 ③

2 ③

3 (e) William and two men who rescued from the first trip
→ William and two men who were rescued from the first trip

4 ④

keeper	관리자, 지키는 사람	lighthouse	등대
violent	폭력적인, 격렬한	isolate	고립시키다
steamship	기선, 상선	terrify	무섭게 하다
notify	알리다	immediately	즉시, 당장
set out	시작하다, 착수하다	rescue	구조하다
against	반대하여	risk	~을 위험에 내맡기다
worn out	기진맥진한	remaining	남아 있는
along with	~와 더불어	Royal Humane Society	영국 수난 구조회
courageous	용감한, 용기 있는	humane act	인도적[훌륭한] 행위
tuberculosis	결핵(증)	courage	용기
insatiable	만족할 줄 모르는	brutal	잔인한
accommodation	숙소, 적응	heroine	여자 영웅

WORD REVIEW p.58

A

1	thinker	14	deforest
2	ruler	15	current rate
3	Confucianism	16	alternative energy
4	poverty	17	keeper
5	advertisement	18	isolate
6	manufacturer	19	humane act
7	intend to	20	set out
8	exclusively	21	relatively
9	obey	22	means
10	necessarily	23	carbon dioxide
11	composer	24	replace
12	satisfaction	25	courageous
13	temperature		

B

1	성실한, 충실한	14	화석 연료
2	신중한, 분별 있는	15	축소하다, 줄어들다
3	사려 깊은	16	구조하다, 구조
4	헌신하다	17	등대
5	제품, 상품	18	무섭게 하다
6	비용 효율이 높은	19	기진맥진한
7	~할 것 같다	20	~와 함께, 더불어
8	알리다	21	보장
9	탐험하다	22	방출
10	~에 대해 언급하다	23	~에 대해 비난하다
11	방출하다	24	확장하는, 팽창하는
12	결과적으로	25	~에 반대하여
13	빙산		

C

| 1 | ④ | 3 | ④ |
| 2 | ④ | | |

D

1 이 장난감들은 나의 친척들이 준건데, 그들은 나와 함께 산다.

2 이것은 사람들이 인터넷 쇼핑을 하는 동안 자선기관에 기부를 할 수 있게 하는 새로운 방법이다.

3 Those who never make it

E	1	④		3	③
	2	④			

F	1	b, e		4	f, h
	2	c, g		5	i, j
	3	a, d			

SENTENCE REVIEW p.60

1	speaking	3	than → of
2	doesn't		

Chapter 04

Mini Quiz p.62

1	e	7	ongoing
2	d	8	mighty
3	f	9	meditation
4	b	10	vital
5	a	11	broadcasted
6	c	12	categorized

Reading Skill p.63

③ 그것을 하기 위해 이용할 수 있는 시간

Unit 01 p.64

1	④		2	(1) True (2) False (3) False

Buddhist	불교도	meditation	명상, 묵상
karma	업보(業報), 인과응보, 숙명	Nirvana	열반, 극락
define	정의를 내리다	mistreat	혹사하다, 학대하다
Buddha	석가모니	prevalence	보급, 널리 퍼짐
worship	숭배하다	religious	종교적인
moral	도덕적인	force	세력, 집단, 단체

Writing & Speaking p.65

1 어린 시절은 모험을 할 나이이다. 비록 오늘날 모험의 기회가 예전보다 상당히 줄기는 했지만, 오늘까지도 이것은 여전히 사실이다.

2 Even though the ghost came into the room, we did not scream.

Unit 02 p.66

1	③		2	④

introduction	도입	guarantee	보증하다
vital	중요한	responsiveness	반응성
make up	구성하다	characteristic	특성, 특징
require	~을 필요로 하다	one-size-fits-all strategy 모든 것을 하나의 크기로 맞추는 전략	
emphasis	강조	aspect	측면
categorize	범주화하다	emerging	신흥의, 성장하는
analysis	분석	vastly	거대하게, 엄청나게 크게
be composed of	~로 구성되다	numerous	매우 많은, 수많은

Writing & Speaking p.67

1 당신 자신과 다른 출신 배경을 가진 사람들과 대화를 나누는 것은 당신의 대화 레퍼토리와 생각을 넓히는 데 도움이 될 수 있다.

2 Don't kill the goose that lays the golden eggs.

Unit 03 p.68

1	②		2	③

shorten	줄이다	celebrate	경축하다, 축하하다
harvest	수확(추수)	origin	기원
Celtic	켈트족	deceased	고인, 죽은 사람
placate	달래다, 위로하다	evil spirit	악령
victim	희생자	treat	음식, 먹거리
spooky	무시무시한	combination	결합, 짝 맞추기

Writing & Speaking p.69

1 언어는 사람들이 서로 의사소통을 하기 위해서 존재한다. 그러나 종종 언어는 두 명의 개인 사이에서 그리고 민족들 간의 오해의 소지가 될 수도 있다.

2 The thief wore black so that the people would not recognize him.

Unit 04 p.70

1	②		3	②
2	⑤		4	④

be eager to	~에 열심이다	ethical	윤리의
morality	도덕성, 윤리성	biological	생물학적인
cloning	복제	nothing but	단지 ~일 뿐(only)
human reproductive right 인간 생식의 권리		conduct	수행하다, 실시하다
experimentation	실험(법)	fetus	태아
abnormality	비정상	publish	공식적으로 발표하다
andrology 남성병학 (남성의 병을 연구하는 학문)		ongoing	진행 중인
infertile	생식력이 없는, 불임의	attempt to	~하기를 시도하다
oppose	반대하다	bill	법안, 의안
House of Representatives (미 의회, 주 의회의) 하원		outlaw	금지하다, 불법화하다
offender	위반자	penalize	유죄로 선고하다, 처형하다
tribulation	고난, 시련	species	종
consequence	결과	ban	금지

Unit 05 p.72

1	⑤		3	④
2	④		4	(C) attacking → attack

frightened	겁에 질린	subdue	정복하다
hardcore	강경한, 단호한, 타협하지 않는	Muslim	이슬람교
overthrow	굴복(전복)시키다	rule	지배하다
terrorist	테러리스트, 테러행위자	a good number of	상당히 많은
plot	~을 몰래 계획하다, 음모를 꾸미다	hijack	공중 납치하다
collapse	무너지다, 붕괴하다	due to	~때문에
opposition	반대, 저항, 야당	Opposition Alliance	야당 연맹
defeat	패배시키다	statement	연설, 주장
broadcast	~을 방송하다	subsequently	그 후에
be known by	~에 의해 알려지다	bravery	용감함
mighty	강력한, 강대한	candidate	후보자
ignorance	무지, 무시	sorrow	슬픔
revenge	복수		

SENTENCE REVIEW — p.76

1 The boy sitting next to James said that he could pass the exam because James had helped him a lot with the study.
2 feeling, smelling, buying, knowing
3 anything

Bonus Chapter

WORD REVIEW — p.74

A	1	Buddhist		14	morality
	2	mistreat		15	experimentation
	3	define		16	ongoing
	4	prevalence		17	subdue
	5	introduction		18	opposition
	6	responsiveness		19	hijack
	7	aspect		20	subsequently
	8	be composed of		21	origin
	9	shorten		22	victim
	10	harvest		23	collapse
	11	spooky		24	defeat
	12	religious		25	broadcast
	13	cloning			

B	1	대우하다, 음식		14	생식력이 없는
	2	도덕적인		15	태아
	3	명상		16	윤리적인
	4	숭배하다		17	음모를 꾸미다
	5	특성, 특징		18	단호한, 강경한
	6	보증하다		19	~때문에
	7	~을 필요로 하다		20	연설, 주장
	8	중요한		21	수많은, 다수의
	9	달래다, 위로하다		22	죽은
	10	범주화하다		23	~에 열심이다
	11	분석		24	~하기를 시도하다
	12	강조		25	강력한
	13	수행하다, 실시하다			

C	1	①	3	③
	2	②		

D 1 비록 그는 중대한 실수를 저질렀지만 그는 이 나라를 위해 많은 일을 했다.
2 간단히 말해, 우리는 아이들이 양심, 즉 그들을 옳은 길로 지켜줄 수 있는 내부의 강한 목소리를 키우기를 원한다는 것이다.
3 in order to achieve productive and positive results

E	1	③	3	②
	2	③		

F	1	define	3	aspect
	2	definite	4	inspect

Mini Quiz — p.80

1	f	7	yelled
2	d	8	represent
3	c	9	approximately
4	e	10	axis
5	b	11	assumed
6	a	12	seduce

Reading Skill — p.81

③ 한국인들은 일생 동안 한 직업에 종사하는 경향이 있다.

Unit 01 — p.82

1 ②   2 ④

thinker	사상가	philosopher	철학자
emperor	황제	put it this way	이렇게 말하다
take a nap	낮잠 자다	stinky-smelling	고약한 냄새가 나는
mustache	콧수염	yell	소리치다
examine	살피다, 검사하다	go away	사라지다
desperately	절망적으로, 필사적으로	scent	냄새

Writing & Speaking — p.83

1 확실히 아시아 사람들은 그들이 슬플 때조차도 예의를 지키려고 웃지만, 그러한 행동이 그들에게 특별한 것인지 아닌지 의문이다.
2 The fire fighters did not know if the fire started in the basement or the kitchen.

Unit 02 — p.84

1 ③   2 ②

mermaid	인어	upper body	상반신
resemble	~을(와) 닮다	seduce	유혹하다, 꼬드기다
drown	익사하다	supernatural	초자연의, 신기의
foresee	예견하다	mythical	신화의
exhausted	기진맥진한	mirage	망상, 신기루

assume	가정하다, 추정하다	fin	지느러미

Writing & Speaking — p.85

1 프로그램을 다듬고 개선한 후에, 컴퓨터 공학자들은 그것을 마이크로소프트 회사에 제출할 정도로 자신있었다.

2 Karen was rich enough to tour any country she wished for winter vacation.

Unit 03 — p.86

1 ③　　2 ⑤

order	[생물] (동식물 분류상의) 목(目)	Chiroptera	익수류(翼手類)
approximately	대략, 대체로	comprise	~으로 이루어지다
genera	(genus의 복수) [생물] 속(屬)	mammal	포유류
capable of	~할 수 있는	evolve	진화하다
acoustic	청각의, 음파를 사용하는	orientation	지향, 방위 측정
technical term	전문용어	echolocation	반향 위치 결정법
inhabit	서식하다	resemblance	닮음, 유사함
habitation	거주(지)	endangered	멸종 위기에 처한

Writing & Speaking — p.87

1 어떤 사람들에게 있어서, 외국어로 휴대전화 통화를 하려 하는 것이 어려운 것처럼 보인다. 이러한 어려움에는 정당한 이유가 있다.

2 There is a man who wears only one sock.

Unit 04 — p.88

1 ④　　3 ④
2 ②　　4 ③

claim	주장	recently	최근에
information age	정보시대	misleading	오도하는
flood	범람하다, 가득 차다	incorrectly	부정확하게
ancestor	조상	inhabit	살다, 거주하다
innocent	순진한, 단순한	beyond	~을 넘어서서
valid	타당한, 정당한	assume	추정하다, 추측하다
distinct	다른, 별개의	relatively	상대적으로
come up with	떠오르다, 생각이 나다	primitiveness	원시성, 원시적인 것
confirm	확인하다	fundamentally	근본적으로
constant	지속적인	instant	즉각적인
access to	~에 대한 접근	density	밀도
transmit	전하다, 전송하다	thanks to	~덕분에
satellite	인공위성	instantly	즉각적으로

Unit 05 — p.90

1 ④　　3 ⑤
2 ②　　4 ⑤

circle around	주변을 돌다	measure	재다, 측정하다
depending on	~에 따라서, 의존하여	northern hemisphere	북반구
southern hemisphere	남반구	seasonal	계절에 따른
orbiting motion	공전운동	rotation	회전, 순환
axis	(회전체의) 축	knitting needle	뜨개바늘
represent	상징하다, 나타내다	stick	찔러 넣다, 고정시키다
spin	돌리다, 회전하다	longitudinal	경도의, 경선의
tilt	기울다	slightly	약간
lean	기대다	angle	각도

perpendicular	수직선, 수직의 위치	continuously	지속적으로
vice versa	반대로, 거꾸로	circulation	순환
lunar eclipse	월식	solar eclipse	일식
briefly	간략히		

WORD REVIEW — p.92

A

1	philosopher	14	ancestor
2	yell	15	fundamentally
3	take a nap	16	instantly
4	mustache	17	tilt
5	go away	18	seasonal
6	desperately	19	longitudinal
7	foresee	20	vice versa
8	assume	21	density
9	drown	22	thanks to
10	misleading	23	axis
11	technical term	24	beyond
12	exhausted	25	innocent
13	flood		

B

1	~을(와) 닮다	14	끊임없는
2	~할 수 있는	15	원시성, 원시적인 것
3	멸종 위기에 처한	16	인공위성
4	살펴보다, 검사하다	17	공전운동
5	대략	18	회전, 순환
6	상반신	19	상징하다, 나타내다
7	유혹하다, 꼬드기다	20	주변을 돌다
8	~으로 이루어지다	21	타당한
9	초자연적인	22	떠오르다
10	청각의	23	전하다, 전송하다
11	비슷함	24	지속적으로
12	서식하다	25	기대다
13	다른, 별개의		

C

1 ①　　3 ④
2 ④

D

1 일본의 고령인구가 늘어나는 현상은 그들이 여전히 일을 계속 할 정도로 젊다는 결정을 내리게 했다.

2 부모들이 자식들을 스포츠 캠프에 보낼 때, 코치들이 아이들의 의견을 존중해 주는지 아닌지를 알기 위해 코치들과 이야기를 나눠봐야 한다.

3 There are several reasons why

E

1 ①　　3 ③
2 ①

F

1	transmits	3	consume
2	transformed	4	assume

SENTENCE REVIEW — p.94

1 because → because of　　3 is
2 exhausted